EMPOWERING THE FUTURE

WHY BLACK AMERICANS MUST EMBRACE AI NOW

By Ross Jones

COLEMAN JONES

PRESS

Published by Coleman Jones Press
Boca Raton, FL
www.ColemanJonesPress.us

This is a work of non-fiction. While the author has made
every effort to ensure the accuracy of the information
contained herein, this book is intended to provide general
information and should not be considered as legal, financial,
or professional advice. Readers are encouraged to seek
professional guidance for specific matters.

ISBN: 979-8-30002-830-5

TABLE OF CONTENTS

Introduction   1

Chapter 1
The AI Revolution and the Rhythm of Our Lives   5

Chapter 2
Our Legacy with Technology–A Journey of Innovation,   11
Adversity, and Resilience

Chapter 3
AI as a Beacon for Social and Economic Empowerment   18

Chapter 4
Overcoming Barriers–Unlocking Access to AI Education   27
and Resources

Chapter 5
AI in the Workforce–Embracing Opportunities and   36
Overcoming Challenges

Chapter 6
Entrepreneurship and Innovation in the AI Era   46

Chapter 7
Addressing Bias in AI–The Imperative for Diverse Voices   56

Chapter 8
Building Community Through Technology   65

Chapter 9
Case Studies–Black Innovators in AI   75

Chapter 10
Preparing the Next Generation for an AI-Driven World   84

Chapter 11
Seizing the Moment for a Brighter Future   93

Final Thoughts   99

About The Author   103

Resources   105

FOREWORD

From the very beginning of Ross's journey with AI, I've had the privilege of witnessing his visionary mind in action. Long before ChatGPT made waves, Ross was experimenting with groundbreaking AI tools like Jasper, Sonic, and Ryter, pushing the boundaries of what technology could do for businesses. He's always been ahead of his time, not only advancing his own knowledge but taking others along with him, treating it as a personal mission to make sure they understood the potential of these innovations.

When I started in commercial real estate, Ross was the mastermind behind my journey from a newcomer to a top agent in my market. He showed me how to generate leads in an industry not yet accustomed to digital strategies, transforming not only my business but also my understanding of what was possible. Just as he empowered me, he has gone on to empower countless others.

Ross has impacted a diverse community, from executives and business owners to pastors, ministry leaders, and individuals simply needing a hand up. His mission is always the same: to make success achievable for anyone, no matter where they are in life. It's not just his deep understanding of AI and digital marketing that sets him apart; it's his drive to share that knowledge generously, ensuring everyone around him has a path to thrive.

In **Empowering the Future**, Ross speaks to a vision of success that's accessible to anyone, at any level. For many in the Black community especially, he champions a new reality: gone are the days of feeling held back or searching in the dark for answers the playing field has been leveled, and with AI as a tool, the only limits are the ones we set for ourselves. There are no excuses—no lack of education, or blaming external forces for a lack of progress can stand in the way of success. Whether someone wants to build a family legacy, start a business, climb the corporate ladder, or simply create a better life, Ross shows us it's now possible and easier than ever before. With AI, the sky is truly the limit.

This book is more than a guide to using AI; it's a call to rise above, embrace the opportunities technology offers, and rewrite the narrative of what's possible. I'm proud to introduce you to *Empowering the Future* and to the brilliant, generous mind behind it. Ross is a visionary, yes—but more importantly, he has a heart for people and a passion for those seeking transformation. He challenges and inspires us all to reach higher and believe in what's possible.

So dive in, take notes, and be inspired, as Ross shares insights sure to inspire and guide you in creating the future you envision. I truly believe the best is yet to come.

Here's to your success,

Tracee Jones

Tracee Jones, Managing Partner
CommercialRealEstateMarketing.com

INTRODUCTION

A Legacy of Resilience and the Dawn of a New Era

Artificial Intelligence (AI) is no longer a distant concept confined to the realms of science fiction; it is a transformative force reshaping industries, economies, and societies across the globe. For Black Americans, the emergence of AI presents a pivotal moment filled with unprecedented opportunities and challenges that we cannot afford to ignore. This book is a call to action—a journey exploring why embracing AI now is crucial for our communities throughout the United States.

AI technologies are seamlessly integrated into our daily lives—from the personalized recommendations we receive on streaming services to the advanced algorithms steering financial markets. As these technologies evolve, they hold the potential to either bridge or widen the social and economic gaps that have long existed. The choice is ours. The key lies in proactive engagement, education, and participation.

> **"I know of no time in human history where ignorance was better than knowledge."**
>
> – *Neil deGrasse Tyson*

A Tribute to Those Who Paved the Way

My story begins with two extraordinary individuals who shaped my life and instilled in me the values of resilience, innovation, and determination—my parents. My mother was one of the most gifted registered nurses to emerge from our hometown of Bunnell, Florida, perhaps even all of Florida. Driven and dedicated, she often worked double shifts, her intelligence and innovative spirit touching countless lives.

When I was eight years old, a near-tragic accident at my father's garage, Jones Automotive, left me with severe burns on my forehead. I had been warming myself by a 55-gallon drum burning wood during the winter when I decided to slide a combustible part into the fire using an empty cardboard box. It exploded, narrowly missing my eyes but badly burning my forehead.

The doctors wanted to treat me in a way that would have left a tremendous scar. But my mother, always ahead of her time, had read about a new treatment using cocoa butter and allowing the wound to heal naturally in the air. She chose this path, and it worked—saving me from a lifelong scar and teaching me the power of knowledge and innovation.

She had us taking vitamins before they were commonplace in our community, always emphasizing the importance of health and well-being. Whether working in emergency rooms, ICUs, eldercare, or with young adults facing mental health challenges, she not only provided exceptional care but also guided countless younger nurses in finding direction in their careers. She was a pillar of strength, a supportive wife to my father, and an empowering mother.

Yet, she had one flaw that cost her greatly. As technology advanced, she wasn't a fan of smartphones or email. When schedules and essential communications moved to digital platforms, her reluctance to adapt forced her into an earlier retirement than she had planned. It was a poignant reminder of how the rapid pace of technological change can impact even the most talented among us.

My father was an amazingly inventive and creative mechanic. He was one of the first Black businessmen to establish himself in the predominantly white part of Bunnell, Florida—a bold move that was met with hostility. The Ku Klux Klan vandalized his garage, breaking windows and making threats. But we prevailed. His determination pushed the business forward despite the adversity.

He always wanted to learn how to use computers but never had the opportunity due to the demands of raising and providing for eight children. Yet, he had the foresight to introduce me to my first computer—a great sacrifice that I now realize was his way of investing in my future. By the grace of God, his vision is being fulfilled in me.

This book is a dedication to my mother and father, and to all those who came before us with dreams and desires but lacked the resources to realize them fully. It is a testament to their sacrifices and a guide for how we can honor their legacy by embracing the opportunities before us. May this book open doors to a greater destiny through knowledge and inspire us to reach heights they only imagined.

Rewriting Our Narrative Through AI

Historically, Black Americans have faced systemic barriers in accessing quality education, employment opportunities, and technological resources. But the digital age offers us a chance to rewrite this narrative. By embracing AI, we can harness tools that promote economic empowerment, social justice, and community development. We can ensure that we are not just spectators in this technological revolution but active participants and leaders.

This book delves into the multifaceted relationship between Black Americans and AI. We will discuss our historical context, examine current challenges, and, most importantly, highlight pathways to leverage AI for positive change. The time to act is now; delaying our engagement with AI could result in missed opportunities and widened inequalities.

Join Me on This Journey

I invite you to join me as we navigate this critical landscape. Together, we'll explore how we can transform challenges into opportunities, turning the very tools that could hinder us into instruments of empowerment. Let us step boldly into this revolutionary field—not just as consumers of AI technologies but as innovators, contributors, and leaders shaping the future we want to see.

Our ancestors laid the groundwork with their resilience and vision. It's our turn to build upon that foundation, harnessing the power of AI to create a legacy of prosperity, equality, and innovation for generations to come.

CHAPTER 1
The AI Revolution and the Rhythm of Our Lives

I can still recall the hum of excitement that filled the room when I booted up my first computer, the Commodore 64. The thrill of watching lines of code transform into simple games wasn't just about entertainment—it was about possibility.

Those early moments ignited a passion for technology that has carried me through life, allowing me to witness and participate in some of the most transformative advancements of our time. Today, Artificial Intelligence (AI) stands as the latest frontier, poised to revolutionize every facet of our existence.

Understanding Artificial Intelligence
Breathing Life into Machines

Imagine teaching a child to recognize patterns, make decisions, and understand language. Now, envision doing the same with a machine. That's the essence of AI—creating systems that perform tasks typically requiring human intelligence. It's more than just cold code and algorithms; it's about infusing technology with the ability to learn and adapt.

Consider the joy of discovering a new favorite song because a streaming service understood your taste, or the convenience of receiving personalized recommendations when shopping online. These everyday experiences are powered by AI, seamlessly woven into the fabric of our lives. It's not just about machines doing tasks; it's about enhancing human experiences, making our lives richer and more connected.

A GLOBAL ECONOMIC TAPESTRY
Weaving Opportunities for All

The economic implications of AI are vast and profound. According to the McKinsey Global Institute, AI could contribute a staggering $13 trillion to the global economy by 2030. But what does that mean for us?

Picture a bustling marketplace, not just of goods, but of ideas and innovations. AI is the loom weaving this new economic tapestry, creating industries we hadn't imagined a decade ago. For Black Americans, this represents a golden opportunity to carve out a significant presence in burgeoning fields. Our unique perspectives, creativity, and resilience can drive innovation in ways that not only benefit us but society as a whole.

Think of entrepreneurs like Tristan Walker, who founded Walker & Company Brands to meet the unique grooming needs of people of color. By leveraging technology and understanding his community's needs, he built a successful company that was later acquired by Procter & Gamble. His story illustrates how recognizing a gap and filling it with innovation can lead to remarkable success.

SOCIETAL SHIFTS
Bridging or Widening the Divide?

AI holds the promise of bridging existing social and economic gaps by providing tools and opportunities previously out of reach. For instance, AI-driven educational platforms can offer personalized learning experiences to students in underserved communities, leveling the playing field. Medical diagnostics powered by AI can improve healthcare access and outcomes for those who have historically been marginalized.

However, there's a flip side. Without intentional engagement, AI risks widening these gaps, exacerbating inequalities that have long plagued our communities. Automated systems can perpetuate biases if they're built without diverse input, leading to unfair practices in hiring, lending, or law enforcement.

Consider the case of facial recognition technology misidentifying individuals of color at disproportionately higher rates. This isn't just a technical glitch; it's a societal concern that can lead to wrongful arrests or surveillance. It's a stark reminder that if we're not at the table, we're likely on the menu.

"Technology is a double-edged sword. It will either empower you or it will disempower you. The choice is yours."

– Anonymous

THE DIGITAL DIVIDE
Answering the Call to Action

Historically, our communities have faced systemic barriers to accessing quality education, employment opportunities, and technological resources. I recall visiting a school in a predominantly Black neighborhood where the computer lab consisted of outdated machines barely capable of running basic programs. Meanwhile, just a few miles away, students had access to the latest technology, robotics clubs, and coding classes. This disparity isn't just about equipment; it's about the opportunities those tools unlock.

Bridging the digital divide is more than providing devices and internet access; it's about investing in our future. It's ensuring that our children grow up not just as consumers of technology but as creators and innovators. It's about empowering a generation to not only use AI but to shape it.

REPRESENTATION MATTERS
Building Fairer Technologies

Diversity in AI development isn't just a nice-to-have; it's a necessity. When diverse voices contribute to creating technology, we produce solutions that are more equitable and reflective of our society's rich tapestry.

Take Dr. Joy Buolamwini, a computer scientist and digital activist who discovered that facial recognition software couldn't accurately detect her face due to her skin tone. Her research led to the founding of the Algorithmic Justice.

League, aiming to combat bias in AI. Her work underscores the critical importance of representation in technology—without it, we risk developing tools that inadvertently harm the very communities they should serve.

By increasing our presence in AI development, we ensure that the technologies shaping our future consider the nuances of all experiences. We can embed ethics, fairness, and empathy into AI, crafting tools that uplift rather than undermine.

AI IN OUR EVERYDAY LIVES
The Invisible Thread

AI is often invisible, quietly enhancing our daily routines. When you use a navigation app to find the quickest route home, AI algorithms analyze traffic patterns in real-time. Virtual assistants schedule appointments, answer questions, and even help manage our homes. In healthcare, AI assists doctors in diagnosing diseases earlier and more accurately.

Consider how AI-powered applications are transforming eldercare. For instance, there are apps that help elderly individuals manage their medication schedules. These apps send reminders, track dosages, and can even alert family members or caregivers if a dose is missed. This technology provides peace of mind for families and improves the quality of life for our elders.

Understanding these applications empowers us to make informed decisions. We can advocate for technologies that serve our communities, address specific challenges we face, and ensure that AI's benefits are accessible to all.

Embracing Our Role in the AI Revolution

The AI revolution is not a distant future; it's happening now, and its impact is profound. For Black Americans, this is a pivotal moment—an opportunity to harness AI for empowerment, innovation, and equity.

Imagine a future where our businesses thrive by leveraging AI to reach new markets, where our children learn in classrooms enhanced by personalized AI tutors, and where healthcare disparities are reduced through AI-driven diagnostics and treatments tailored to our needs.

But this future isn't guaranteed. It requires us to step forward, to engage proactively, and to lend our voices to the conversation. This book is an invitation to join me on this journey—to explore our historical context, understand the current landscape, and envision a future where AI serves as a catalyst for positive change in our communities.

Together, let's embrace AI not just as a tool but as a partner. Let's be the innovators, the decision-makers, and the leaders who shape AI's trajectory. By doing so, we can build a brighter, more equitable future for all.

CHAPTER 2
Our Legacy with Technology—A Journey of Innovation, Adversity, and Resilience

As we delve into the story of technology and Black Americans, it's essential to recognize that our relationship with innovation is deeply rooted in a history of perseverance and ingenuity. This legacy is not just about gadgets and machines; it's about the spirit of a people who have consistently turned obstacles into opportunities.

Understanding this historical relationship is crucial to appreciating why embracing AI today is not just an option but a continuation of our enduring legacy.

EARLY PIONEERS
Lighting the Way with Ingenuity

Long before the digital age, Black Americans were making significant strides in technological innovation. Consider Granville T. Woods, often hailed as the "Black Edison." In the late 19th and early 20th centuries, Woods patented numerous electrical devices that laid the groundwork for modern railway systems. His inventions, including the multiplex telegraph and the third rail for electric trains, revolutionized transportation and communication.

Woods' story is one of relentless determination. Despite facing racial discrimination and limited access to formal education, he taught himself engineering and went on to register nearly 60 patents. His contributions not only advanced technology but also inspired future generations to believe in their potential to shape the world.

Another remarkable figure is Madam C.J. Walker, the first self-made female millionaire in America. While not an inventor in the traditional sense, she harnessed the power of entrepreneurship and innovation by developing a line of hair care products for Black women. Her success story illustrates how understanding and addressing the unique needs of our community can lead to groundbreaking achievements.

NAVIGATING SYSTEMIC BARRIERS
The Persistent Digital Divide

Despite these early successes, Black Americans have historically faced significant obstacles in accessing education, employment, and technological resources. Segregation, economic disparities, and discriminatory practices created a digital divide that limited our ability to fully participate in technological advancements—a gap that, unfortunately, echoes into the present day.

In many predominantly Black communities, schools often received less funding, resulting in outdated technology and fewer opportunities for students to engage with emerging technologies. There are stories of schools where textbooks were hand-me-downs from better-funded districts, and science labs were practically non-existent. This lack of access hindered our ability to compete on an equal footing, creating barriers that we are still striving to overcome.

TECHNOLOGY AS A TOOL FOR SOCIAL CHANGE
Amplifying Our Voices

Throughout history, we have leveraged technology as a means to amplify our voices and advocate for justice. During the civil rights movement of the 1950s and 1960s, television played a pivotal role in broadcasting the harsh realities of segregation and brutality to a wider audience.

Images of peaceful protesters being met with violence stirred the conscience of the nation and the world, galvanizing support for change.

In recent years, the rise of social media has become a powerful tool in movements like Black Lives Matter. Platforms such as Twitter, Instagram, and Facebook have provided unprecedented opportunities for organizing, sharing stories, and fostering solidarity. Hashtags like #BlackLivesMatter and #SayHerName have brought attention to injustices that might have otherwise gone unnoticed, highlighting the critical role technology plays in modern activism.

BUILDING THE BLACK TECH COMMUNITY
A Growing Presence

The tech industry has long been criticized for its lack of diversity, but there is a growing presence of Black professionals making waves in this field. Organizations like **Black Girls CODE**, founded by Kimberly Bryant, are instrumental in empowering and connecting Black individuals in technology. Bryant's vision was inspired by her daughter, who loved video games but felt isolated as one of the few girls—and even fewer Black girls—in her coding classes. Black Girls CODE offers workshops and programs that teach young Black girls the fundamentals of programming and computer science. By providing these educational opportunities, we are nurturing the next generation of tech leaders and ensuring that our perspectives are represented in the technologies that shape our world.

Events like **AfroTech** bring together thousands of Black tech professionals and entrepreneurs, creating a space for networking, collaboration, and showcasing innovation. These initiatives foster a sense of community that is crucial for encouraging participation and success in tech.

OVERCOMING WORKPLACE CHALLENGES
Bias, Mentorship, and Education

Despite progress, Black Americans remain underrepresented in the tech workforce. This underrepresentation is often exacerbated by workplace bias, limited access to mentorship, and educational gaps. Subtle and overt discrimination can impede career advancement, making it challenging for Black professionals to ascend to leadership positions or secure roles in cutting-edge fields.

For instance, studies have shown that resumes with traditionally Black-sounding names receive fewer callbacks than identical resumes with white-sounding names. Such biases highlight the systemic issues that continue to affect employment opportunities.

Moreover, the lack of role models and mentors in the industry can diminish interest and perceived accessibility for aspiring Black technologists. Educational disparities, particularly in STEM fields, further limit preparedness for AI and technology roles. Addressing these challenges requires a multifaceted approach, including advocating for inclusive hiring practices, creating mentorship opportunities, and ensuring equitable access to quality education.

RESILIENCE AND ADAPTATION
Leveraging Technology for Entrepreneurship and Activism

Throughout history, Black Americans have continuously adapted to technological changes, leveraging new tools for entrepreneurship, education, and activism. The internet and social media have been particularly instrumental in fostering movements and building businesses that cater to our unique needs and interests.

Consider the rise of platforms like Blavity, founded by Morgan DeBaun. Recognizing the lack of media representation for Black millennials, DeBaun created a space that delivers content tailored to our experiences. **Blavity** has grown into a network that includes conferences, events, and additional platforms, demonstrating how understanding and leveraging technology can lead to significant impact.

Similarly, entrepreneurs like Angela Benton, founder of **NewME** (now part of Lightship Capital), have been at the forefront of supporting Black tech founders. By providing resources, mentorship, and access to capital, such initiatives help break down barriers that have historically limited our participation in the tech startup ecosystem.

INCLUSIVITY IN TECH DEVELOPMENT
Ensuring Fair and Reflective Technologies

Involving diverse perspectives in technology development is essential for creating products and services that meet the needs of all users. Inclusivity leads to innovation and better problem-solving, as diverse teams bring a variety of experiences and viewpoints to the table.

Companies are beginning to recognize the value of diversity, but there is still much work to be done. By participating in AI development, Black Americans can help create more fair and

unbiased technologies. Our unique insights can guide the creation of AI systems that are not only effective but also equitable, ensuring they serve the diverse populations they are designed for.

For example, **Dr. Timnit Gebru**, a prominent researcher in AI ethics, has been a leading voice in highlighting how biases in AI can perpetuate discrimination. Her work emphasizes the importance of having diverse voices in tech to identify and address these critical issues.

Building on a Legacy of Innovation and Resilience

The historical relationship between Black Americans and technology is marked by both challenges and triumphs. Acknowledging past obstacles highlights the importance of proactive engagement with AI and emerging technologies. Embracing AI is not just about keeping up with the latest trends; it's about honoring our legacy of innovation and resilience.

As we look ahead, it's clear that our past experiences have equipped us with the knowledge and determination needed to navigate the AI-driven landscape. By leveraging our strengths, addressing systemic barriers, and fostering a supportive community, we can harness AI as a tool for empowerment. Together, we can create a future that not only honors our heritage but also paves the way for new possibilities and achievements.

Our journey with technology is a testament to our resilience and capacity for innovation. By understanding our history and actively shaping our future, we ensure that the legacy we leave is one of empowerment and progress. The time is now to embrace AI and continue the story our ancestors began, turning challenges into stepping stones toward a brighter tomorrow.

CHAPTER 3
AI as a Beacon for Social and Economic Empowerment

Imagine standing at the crossroads of history, where technology offers us a lantern to illuminate paths previously shrouded in darkness. Artificial Intelligence (AI) holds immense potential to transform societies and economies, and for Black Americans, it can be a powerful tool to bridge gaps that have long existed due to systemic inequalities.

Embracing AI isn't just about keeping pace with technology—it's about harnessing it to foster growth, enhance opportunities, and uplift our communities.

ECONOMIC OPPORTUNITIES THROUGH AI
Carving Our Place in the Future

AI technologies are creating new industries and reshaping existing ones at an unprecedented pace. By acquiring AI-related skills, we can access high-paying jobs in sectors like technology, healthcare, finance, and beyond. The demand for AI professionals is soaring, and there aren't enough qualified candidates to fill these roles.

- **Job Creation:** AI is expected to create 2.3 million jobs by 2025, surpassing the number of jobs displaced by automation. This isn't just a statistic; it's a gateway to prosperity for those prepared to seize it.

- **Entrepreneurship:** AI opens avenues for startups and

small businesses to innovate and compete on a global scale. Think of innovators like **Rodney Williams**, co-founder of LISNR, a company that uses ultrasonic audio technology for data transmission. His work demonstrates how combining creativity with cutting-edge technology can lead to groundbreaking solutions.

- **Investment Opportunities:** Knowledge of AI can lead to informed investment decisions in emerging technologies and markets. By understanding AI trends, we can participate in wealth-building opportunities that have historically been out of reach.

Consider the story of **Ida Byrd-Hill**, the founder of **Automation Workz**, a cybersecurity reskilling firm focusing on underrepresented populations. Recognizing the looming threat of automation displacing workers, she created an organization that equips individuals with the skills needed for the future. Her efforts not only empower people with jobs but also contribute to diversifying the tech industry.

EDUCATION AND SKILL DEVELOPMENT
Unlocking the Door to Empowerment

Access to AI education is crucial for empowerment. Educational programs and initiatives focused on AI can equip us with the skills needed to thrive in the digital economy. This includes coding bootcamps, online courses, and university programs tailored to make learning accessible.

> "Education is the most powerful weapon which you can use to change the world."

> — *Nelson Mandela*

Organizations like **Hidden Genius Project** in Oakland, California, work tirelessly to increase representation by providing mentorship and training in technology creation, entrepreneurship, and leadership skills to Black male youth. By investing in education, we're not just teaching skills—we're igniting hope and possibility.

Imagine community centers offering AI and coding classes to youth and adults alike, transforming neighborhoods into hubs of innovation. By investing in education, we're unlocking doors to opportunities that can change lives.

AI FOR SOCIAL JUSTICE
A Tool for Change

AI can be harnessed to address social issues and promote justice. Its applications have the potential to uncover hidden patterns, inform policy, and drive meaningful change.

- **Predictive Analytics:** By analyzing data, AI can identify social disparities in areas like housing, education, and healthcare. This information can guide policymakers in allocating resources more equitably.

- **Criminal Justice Reform:** AI tools can detect biases in legal systems, such as disparities in sentencing or policing practices. Organizations are developing algorithms to promote fairer outcomes and reduce systemic racism.

- **Community Development:** AI can assist in urban planning and resource allocation, helping to improve living conditions in underserved communities. For example, AI-driven models can optimize public transportation routes to better serve areas lacking access.

Consider the work of **Data for Black Lives**, a movement of activists and data scientists who use data science to fight discrimination and promote justice. By leveraging AI and data analytics, they aim to empower communities and influence policy changes.

HEALTHCARE ADVANCEMENTS
Healing Our Communities

AI has the potential to revolutionize healthcare, greatly benefiting Black communities that often face health disparities.

- **Personalized Medicine:** AI can tailor treatments based on individual genetic profiles, improving effectiveness and reducing adverse effects.

- **Disease Prevention:** Early detection of conditions prevalent in our communities, such as hypertension and diabetes, can save lives. AI algorithms can analyze medical images and patient data to spot warning signs that might be missed otherwise.

- **Accessibility:** Telemedicine powered by AI increases access to healthcare services, particularly in areas lacking medical facilities. Virtual consultations and AI-driven diagnostic tools bring healthcare to our fingertips.

Imagine AI applications that monitor heart health through wearable devices, alerting users to potential issues before they become critical. These technologies empower individuals to take charge of their health, bridging gaps in healthcare access.

FINANCIAL INCLUSION
Building Wealth and Stability

AI-driven financial technologies (FinTech) can promote financial inclusion by providing tools and services that were previously inaccessible.

- **Access to Credit:** Alternative credit scoring using AI can help those without traditional credit histories secure loans, opening doors to homeownership and entrepreneurship.

- **Budgeting Tools:** AI-powered apps assist in managing personal finances effectively, offering personalized advice to help users save and invest wisely.

- **Investment Platforms:** Robo-advisors and micro-investing apps democratize investment opportunities, allowing individuals to grow wealth with small contributions.

Consider platforms like **Freddie**, a financial wellness app founded by **Freddie Figgers**, which uses AI to help users manage their finances, reduce debt, and build credit. By lowering the barriers to financial tools, they make financial stability accessible to a broader audience.

EMPOWERING BUSINESSES
Elevating Black Entrepreneurship

AI-driven financial technologies (FinTech) can promote financial inclusion by providing tools and services that were previously inaccessible.

Black-owned businesses can leverage AI to enhance their operations and competitiveness.

- **Customer Insights:** AI analytics provide a deeper understanding of customer behavior, enabling businesses to tailor products and services effectively.

- **Process Automation:** Streamlining operations through AI reduces costs and increases efficiency, freeing up resources to focus on growth and innovation.

- **Marketing Strategies:** Personalized marketing driven by AI increases engagement and sales by reaching the right customers with the right message.

Imagine a Black-owned beauty brand using AI to analyze market trends and customer feedback, allowing them to develop products that meet the specific needs of their community. By embracing AI, businesses can compete on a larger scale, amplifying their impact.

CULTURAL REPRESENTATION IN AI
Telling Our Stories

By participating in AI development, we ensure that our

culture and experiences are represented accurately and respectfully in AI applications.

- **Content Creation:** AI can be used to create culturally relevant content in media and entertainment. For instance, algorithms can help produce music, art, or literature that reflects diverse perspectives.

- **Language Processing:** Developing AI that understands diverse dialects and languages ensures inclusivity. This is vital for voice recognition systems and translation services that serve our communities.

- **Art and Music:** AI tools can assist artists and musicians in exploring new creative avenues, blending technology with tradition to produce innovative works.

Consider projects like **Beat Machine**, an AI-powered music tool that helps artists create unique sounds by blending different genres and cultural influences. By integrating AI with artistic expression, we celebrate our heritage and innovate simultaneously.

CHALLENGES AND CONSIDERATIONS
Navigating with Caution

While AI offers numerous benefits, it's important to be mindful of potential challenges.

- **Bias in AI Systems:** Without careful oversight, AI algorithms can perpetuate existing prejudices. Diverse representation in AI development is crucial to mitigate this risk.

- **Privacy Concerns:** Protecting personal data is essential. As AI systems collect and analyze vast amounts of information, robust safeguards must be in place to prevent misuse.

- **Accessibility:** Making AI resources and education accessible to all members of the community is vital. Efforts must be made to ensure that technological advancements don't widen existing gaps.

Harnessing AI for Collective Empowerment

AI stands as a powerful tool for social and economic empowerment. By embracing AI, we unlock new opportunities, drive innovation, and contribute to shaping a more equitable future.

Imagine a world where our children attend schools enriched with AI-driven learning tools, where healthcare is personalized and accessible, where businesses thrive by leveraging technology, and where social justice is advanced through data-driven advocacy.

This vision isn't a distant dream—it's within our reach. By actively participating in the AI revolution, we not only benefit ourselves but strengthen our communities and pave the way for the next generation.

Let us seize this moment to harness AI as a beacon, guiding us toward a future of empowerment, prosperity, and unity. Together, we can transform challenges into stepping stones, lighting the path for those who will follow in our footsteps.

As we continue our journey, we'll explore how to overcome barriers to AI education and resources, ensuring that everyone has the opportunity to participate in this transformative field.

The road ahead is filled with possibilities, and by walking it together, we amplify our impact and honor the legacy of those who paved the way.

CHAPTER 4
Overcoming Barriers—Unlocking Access to
AI Education and Resources

Imagine a young student in a bustling city neighborhood, eyes wide with curiosity as they gaze at the stars, dreaming of what lies beyond. Now picture another student in a rural town, tinkering with whatever gadgets they can find, fueled by an innate desire to understand how things work. Both share a common thread—a passion for learning and a spark that could ignite a future in Artificial Intelligence (AI). Yet, systemic barriers threaten to dim that spark before it can fully shine.

Access to education and resources is fundamental to empowering individuals and communities. For Black Americans, overcoming barriers to AI education is crucial to ensure participation in the rapidly evolving digital economy. This chapter explores the challenges we face and the strategies to overcome them, paving the way for equitable access to AI opportunities.

UNDERSTANDING THE BARRIERS
Navigating the Obstacles

Several systemic obstacles hinder access to AI education and resources in our communities:

Educational Inequities
Underfunded schools often lack the necessary technology and qualified educators to teach AI and related subjects.

In many urban and rural areas, students attend schools where computer labs are outdated or nonexistent.

Imagine trying to learn coding on a computer that barely runs or not having access to one at all. This technological gap creates a significant disadvantage.

Economic Constraints
The cost of higher education and specialized training programs can be prohibitive. For many families, affording tuition, books, and living expenses is a daunting challenge. This financial barrier limits access to universities and programs that offer AI education.

Digital Divide
Limited access to high-speed internet and modern devices impedes learning opportunities. In an era where information is at our fingertips, not having reliable internet access is like being cut off from the world. This divide disproportionately affects Black communities, both in urban and rural settings.

Representation Gap
A lack of role models in AI fields can diminish interest and perceived accessibility. When students don't see people who look like them in certain professions, it's harder to envision themselves in those roles. This invisibility can dampen aspirations and deter talented minds from pursuing AI.

STRATEGIES FOR OVERCOMING EDUCATIONAL BARRIERS
Charting the Path Forward

Addressing these challenges requires a multifaceted approach involving individuals, communities, educational institutions, and policymakers.

Community Initiatives: Grassroots Empowerment
Grassroots organizations play a vital role in bridging the education gap.

- **After-School Programs:** Community centers and churches can offer coding and AI workshops to students. For example, the Hidden Genius Project in Oakland empowers young Black men by providing training and mentorship in technology, entrepreneurship, and leadership.

- **Mentorship Opportunities:** Connecting youth with professionals in AI and technology fields can ignite passion and provide guidance. Programs like STEM NOLA, founded by Dr. Calvin Mackie, bring STEM education to communities through hands-on activities and mentorship.

- **Resource Centers:** Establishing community centers equipped with computers and internet access creates safe spaces for learning. These hubs can serve as gateways to knowledge for those without resources at home.

Educational Reforms: Advocating for Systemic Change
Advocating for changes in education can lead to long-term improvements.

- **Curriculum Development:** Incorporating AI and computer science into school curricula ensures all students are exposed to these fields. Schools like Ron Clark Academy in Atlanta integrate technology into their teaching methods, demonstrating what's possible with innovative approaches.

- **Teacher Training:** Equipping educators with the skills to teach AI concepts effectively is crucial. Professional development programs can prepare teachers to inspire the next generation of technologists.

- **Funding Allocation:** Ensuring equitable funding for schools in underserved areas can level the playing field. This requires policy advocacy and community engagement to demand fair distribution of resources.

Utilizing Online Resources: Harnessing the Power of the Internet

The internet offers a wealth of free or affordable educational materials.

- **Massive Open Online Courses (MOOCs):** Platforms like **Coursera, edX,** and **Khan Academy** provide courses in AI and machine learning accessible to anyone with an internet connection.

- **Educational YouTube Channels:** Creators like **Mark E. Moore,** founder of **DECODED,** offer engaging content that breaks down complex AI concepts into understandable lessons.

- **Open-Source Communities:** Engaging with communities that share knowledge and resources freely fosters collaboration and learning. Websites like **GitHub** host projects where beginners can contribute and learn from real-world code.

Scholarships and Financial Aid: Breaking Financial Barriers
Financial barriers can be mitigated through scholarships, grants, and other forms of assistance.

- **Academic Scholarships:** Many universities offer scholarships specifically for students pursuing AI and STEM fields. Organizations like the **United Negro College Fund (UNCF)** provide financial support to Black students.

- **Corporate Programs:** Tech companies often have initiatives to support diversity in technology education. For instance, **Google's Computer Science Summer Institute (CSSI)** offers scholarships and programs for underrepresented groups.

- **Government Grants:** Federal and state programs fund education for underrepresented groups, such as the **Pell Grant** and **Minority Science and Engineering Improvement Program (MSEIP)**.

Role of Tech Companies: Building Bridges
Technology companies can contribute significantly to improving access.

- **Partnerships with Schools:** Providing resources and expertise to educational institutions can enhance learning experiences. Microsoft's Technology Education and Literacy in Schools (TEALS) program pairs tech professionals with teachers to team-teach computer science.

- **Internship Programs:** Offering hands-on experience to students from diverse backgrounds helps build skills and networks. Internships at companies like IBM, Apple, and Facebook open doors to future careers.

• **Diversity and Inclusion Initiatives:** Committing to hiring practices that promote representation ensures that workplaces reflect the diversity of society.

Policy Advocacy: Driving Systemic Transformation
Engaging in policy advocacy can lead to broader systemic change.

• **Educational Funding:** Lobbying for increased investment in schools serving Black communities is essential. Grass roots movements can influence policymakers to prioritize education.

• **Technology Infrastructure:** Advocating for improved internet access and technological infrastructure helps bridge the digital divide. Initiatives like the Lifeline Program aim to make communication services more affordable.

• **Regulatory Support:** Supporting policies that encourage diversity in technology sectors promotes inclusion and equal opportunities.

SUCCESS STORIES
Inspiring the Journey

"Black Girls CODE is devoted to showing the world that Black girls can code, and do so much more."

— *Kimberly Bryant, Founder of Black Girls CODE*

Organizations like **Black Girls CODE** and **Code2040** are making significant strides in providing access and opportunities in technology and AI for Black youth. Their success demonstrates what is possible when passion meets opportunity.

Consider the story of **Jerome Foster II**, a young climate justice activist who, at 18, became the youngest-ever White House adviser. He taught himself to code using online resources and founded **TAU VR**, a virtual reality company focusing on social justice issues. His journey exemplifies how determination and access to resources can lead to remarkable achievements.

PERSONAL EMPOWERMENT
Taking the Initiative

Individuals can take proactive steps to overcome barriers.

- **Self-Learning:** Utilizing free resources to learn AI concepts independently empowers self-motivation. Countless tutorials, courses, and forums are available for those eager to learn.

- **Networking:** Building connections with professionals and peers in the field opens doors. Attending conferences, joining online groups, and participating in hackathons can expand one's network.

- **Setting Goals:** Establishing clear objectives and creating action plans to achieve them provides direction. Whether it's completing a certification or building a portfolio project, setting milestones keeps progress on track.

Collective Effort for Equitable Access

Overcoming barriers to AI education and resources is a collective effort that requires dedication, collaboration, and strategic action. By addressing these challenges head-on, we can unlock the full potential of AI as a tool for empowerment, ensuring that no one is left behind in the technological revolution.

Imagine a future where every child, regardless of their zip code, has access to quality education and the resources to explore AI. A future where the tech industry reflects the diversity of our society, and innovation thrives because of it. Let us be the architects of that future.

By working together—individuals, communities, schools, companies, and governments—we can dismantle the barriers that have held us back and pave the way for a new era of opportunity and inclusion.

As we forge ahead, the next chapter will delve into AI in the workforce, exploring the opportunities and challenges that await us.

By understanding the landscape, we can prepare ourselves to not just participate but to lead in the fields that will define our future.

CHAPTER 5
AI in the Workforce—Embracing Opportunities and Overcoming Challenges

Imagine Jamal, a young man from Detroit who grew up watching factories close and jobs disappear. Determined not to become another statistic, he took advantage of community programs that taught coding and AI basics. Today, Jamal works as a data analyst for a tech company, using AI to solve complex problems. His journey reflects a broader narrative—a testament to resilience and the pursuit of opportunity in an ever-changing workforce landscape.

Artificial Intelligence is redefining industries across the globe. For Black Americans, engaging with AI in the workforce presents significant opportunities for advancement, innovation, and economic empowerment. Yet, it also brings challenges that must be addressed to ensure equitable participation. This chapter examines the impact of AI on employment, explores potential career growth, and discusses the hurdles we need to overcome to thrive in this evolving environment.

TRANSFORMATION OF JOB MARKETS
Navigating New Terrain

AI is automating routine tasks, leading to a shift in the types of jobs available. While some roles are becoming obsolete, new positions are emerging that require different skill sets.

- **Automation of Repetitive Tasks:** Jobs involving routine tasks are increasingly automated, affecting sectors like manufacturing, administrative work, and retail. For instance, self-checkout kiosks and automated customer service bots are replacing traditional roles.

- **Emergence of New Roles:** Positions such as AI specialists, data scientists, machine learning engineers, and AI ethicists are in high demand. These roles involve developing, managing, and overseeing AI technologies that drive innovation.

- **Hybrid Jobs:** Roles that combine technical and domain-specific expertise are growing, requiring a blend of skills. For example, in real estate, professionals who understand both property markets and AI can revolutionize how properties are marketed and sold.

Consider my own journey. My wife Tracee and I recognized the transformative power of AI and decided to take a bold step into this new frontier.

We established **CommercialRealEstateMarketing.com, The CRE Marketing Hub,** and **ContentCreationStudios.us** to develop AI-first marketing solutions, content creation services, and AI enablement tools specifically for the commercial real estate sector and other niches.

Our companies have created thousands of realistic AI-generated images, including diverse representations of people of all ages engaged in business, success, and positive lifestyles. By establishing the world's first AI-generated stock image library and custom AI tools for real estate professionals, Tracee and I are not only embracing new roles but also redefining an industry through innovation.

Our journey illustrates what's possible when we embrace AI with vision and determination. By creating innovative solutions that empower others, we are advancing our own success and contributing to the broader goal of uplifting our communities.

OPPORTUNITIES FOR CAREER ADVANCEMENT
Seizing the Moment

Engaging with AI technologies can open doors to lucrative and fulfilling careers.

- **High-Demand Skills:** Proficiency in AI-related skills is highly sought after, often commanding higher salaries. Companies across various industries are eager to hire professionals who can navigate the complexities of AI.

- **Career Mobility:** Skills in AI enable professionals to transition across industries and roles. A background in AI can lead to opportunities in healthcare, finance, education, real estate, and beyond.

- **Entrepreneurial Ventures:** Knowledge of AI can lead to the development of innovative products and services. Entrepreneurs like Ross and Tracee Jones demonstrate how AI can be leveraged to create cutting-edge solutions that address specific industry needs.

Imagine being part of a team that develops an AI app to help small businesses manage marketing campaigns more efficiently, directly contributing to economic growth in your community.

CHALLENGES FACING BLACK AMERICANS
Confronting the Barriers

Despite the opportunities, several challenges hinder full participation in the AI-driven workforce.

Representation Gap: Bridging the Divide
Black professionals are underrepresented in AI and technology fields. This lack of diversity can lead to:

- **Limited Networks:** Fewer connections can impact job opportunities and career advancement. Networking is crucial in the tech industry, and underrepresentation can limit access to influential circles.

- **Isolation:** Being one of the few Black individuals in a workplace can lead to feelings of isolation and decreased job satisfaction.

- **Bias and Discrimination:** Experiencing workplace bias can hinder professional growth. Unconscious biases may affect hiring decisions, promotions, and project assignments.

For example, **Dr. Ruha Benjamin**, a sociologist and professor at Princeton University, explores how racial bias can be embedded in technology. Her work emphasizes the importance of diversity in tech to identify and address such issues.

Skills Gap: Equipping Ourselves for the Future
Access to quality education and training programs is essential.

- **Educational Disparities:** Unequal access to STEM education affects preparedness for AI roles. Schools in underfunded districts may lack resources to teach advanced technology courses.

- **Continuous Learning:** The fast-paced nature of AI requires ongoing skill development. Professionals need opportunities to update their skills regularly to stay relevant.

- **Credential Requirements:** Many AI roles require advanced degrees or certifications, which can be barriers due to cost and accessibility.

Automation Risk: Protecting Vulnerable Jobs

Jobs predominantly held by Black Americans are at higher risk of automation. This includes roles in transportation, logistics, hospitality, and manufacturing. For instance, autonomous vehicles threaten driving jobs—a field where many Black Americans are employed.

STRATEGIES FOR SUCCESS
Paving the Way Forward

Skill Development: Investing in Our Growth

- **STEM Education:** Focusing on science, technology, engineering, and mathematics from an early age builds a strong foundation. Programs like STEM From Dance use dance to engage girls of color in STEM subjects, making learning relatable and fun.

- **Professional Training:** Pursuing certifications and courses in AI and related fields enhances employability. Online platforms like edX and Udemy offer accessible courses, some of which are free or low-cost.

- **Soft Skills:** Developing communication, problem-solving, and leadership skills complements technical abilities, making professionals more versatile and effective in collaborative environments.

Consider how Ross and Tracee Jones continually invest in their own education and skills to stay at the forefront of AI innovation. By doing so, they've been able to create sophisticated AI tools and services that meet the evolving needs of their clients in the commercial real estate sector and beyond.

Networking and Mentorship: Building Bridges

- **Professional Organizations:** Joining groups like the Information Technology Senior Management Forum (ITSMF) connects individuals with peers and mentors in technology leadership roles.

- **Mentorship Programs:** Seeking guidance from experienced professionals provides support and opens doors. Mentorship can offer invaluable insights into navigating career paths and overcoming obstacles.

- **Conferences and Events:** Attending industry events expands networks. Events like Black Tech Week and AfroTech celebrate Black innovators and create spaces for collaboration and learning.

Advocacy and Policy Change: Shaping the Environment

- **Diversity Initiatives:** Encouraging companies to adopt inclusive hiring practices promotes representation. Supporting and participating in diversity programs can lead to more equitable workplaces.

- **Equal Opportunity Laws:** Advocating for enforcement of anti-discrimination laws ensures that biases are addressed legally and ethically.

- **Corporate Accountability:** Holding organizations account able for diversity commitments pushes for real change. Engaging in shareholder activism or supporting advocacy groups can influence corporate policies.

THE ROLE OF COMPANIES
Fostering Inclusive Workplaces

Organizations play a key role in shaping the workforce landscape.

- **Inclusive Hiring:** Implementing strategies to recruit diverse talent widens the pool of ideas and perspectives, fostering innovation.

- **Bias Training:** Educating employees to recognize and combat unconscious bias creates a more equitable environment and improves team dynamics.

- **Career Development:** Providing opportunities for advancement and skill development ensures that all employees can grow and contribute meaningfully.

Companies like **Salesforce** and **Accenture** have made public commitments to diversity and inclusion, investing in training programs and setting measurable goals for representation. Similarly, Ross and Tracee's companies prioritize diversity, ensuring that their AI-generated content reflects a wide range of cultures, ages, and lifestyles. By doing so, they promote inclusivity not just within their team but also in the products and services they offer.

"Companies that embrace diversity and inclusion in all aspects of their business statistically outperform their peers."

— *Josh Bersin, Industry Analyst*

FUTURE OUTLOOK
Embracing Change

The integration of AI into the workforce is expected to continue accelerating.

- **Reskilling and Upskilling:** Lifelong learning will become the norm to keep pace with technological changes. Both employers and employees must invest in continuous education and adaptability.

- **Human-AI Collaboration:** Emphasis on roles where humans and AI work together effectively will grow. Skills like creativity, emotional intelligence, and strategic thinking will be highly valued.

- **Ethical Considerations:** Growing importance of ethics in

AI development and deployment opens new career paths. Roles focused on AI ethics, governance, and policy are emerging, offering opportunities to shape how AI impacts society.

Imagine a future where AI enhances human capabilities rather than replaces them. In marketing, for instance, AI can handle data analysis and automation, while professionals focus on strategy, creativity, and building client relationships. This synergy is exemplified by Ross and Tracee's approach, where AI tools augment human expertise to deliver exceptional results.

Navigating the AI-Driven Workforce

AI presents a transformative opportunity in the workforce for Black Americans. By addressing challenges and leveraging opportunities, we can position ourselves for success in an AI-driven economy. Collective efforts from individuals, communities, and organizations are essential to ensure that the workforce of the future is inclusive and equitable.

Now is the time to embrace the possibilities, invest in our skills, and break down the barriers that stand in our way. By doing so, we not only advance ourselves but also contribute to a richer, more diverse technological landscape that benefits everyone.

Let us take inspiration from those who have forged paths before us and commit to paving new ones for those who will follow. The AI revolution is here, and with it comes the chance to redefine our futures.

In the next chapter, we'll delve into entrepreneurship and innovation in the AI era, exploring how embracing AI can empower us to create, lead, and build ventures that not only succeed but also uplift our communities.

CHAPTER 6
Entrepreneurship and Innovation in the AI Era

Imagine walking through a neighborhood where once-empty storefronts now buzz with activity–tech startups founded by local entrepreneurs solving problems unique to their community. Artificial Intelligence (AI) is at the heart of this transformation, offering unprecedented opportunities for innovation and economic empowerment. For Black Americans, embracing entrepreneurship in the AI era is more than a business endeavor; it's a pathway to shaping our future and uplifting our communities.

THE AI-DRIVEN ENTREPRENEURIAL LANDSCAPE
A New Frontier

AI technologies are revolutionizing industries by automating processes, enhancing decision-making, and creating new business models. Entrepreneurs leveraging AI can:

- **Identify Market Gaps:** Use AI analytics to uncover unmet consumer needs. For example, by analyzing social media trends and consumer feedback, entrepreneurs can identify products or services that are in demand but not yet available.

- **Optimize Operations:** Implement AI solutions to improve efficiency and reduce costs. AI can automate routine tasks, allowing businesses to focus on strategic growth.

- **Innovate Products and Services:** Develop AI-powered

offerings that address specific problems. From personalized healthcare apps to AI-driven educational tools, the possibilities are vast.

Consider the story of Courtney and Tye Caldwell, founders of ShearShare, an app that connects salon and barbershop owners with stylists looking to rent space. By leveraging AI to match supply and demand efficiently, they've created a platform that addresses a real need in the beauty industry. Their innovative approach demonstrates how technology can transform traditional industries.

OPPORTUNITIES FOR BLACK ENTREPRENEURS
Leading the Charge

There is a significant opportunity for Black entrepreneurs to lead in AI innovation:

- **Niche Markets:** Creating AI solutions tailored to the needs of Black communities. For instance, developing financial tools that address the specific challenges faced by under banked populations.

- **Cultural Insights:** Leveraging cultural understanding to develop relevant technologies. Entrepreneurs who understand their community's unique preferences can create products that resonate more deeply.

- **Social Impact Ventures:** Establishing businesses that address social issues using AI. This includes tackling challenges like healthcare disparities, educational gaps, and economic inequality.

Let me share how Tracee and I navigated this path. Recognizing the potential to revolutionize the commercial real estate industry, we leveraged our cultural insights and understanding of AI to create solutions tailored to our community's needs. By developing AI-powered marketing tools and content creation services, we addressed specific challenges within the industry and provided innovative solutions.

Creating the first ever AI Generated image Library reflecting a diversity of races and cultures that exist in todays commercial real estate business environment that is often underrepresented.

Our work not only demonstrates the possibilities within AI entrepreneurship but also highlights how we, as Black entrepreneurs, can lead in creating technologies that resonate with and uplift our communities.

Also consider DeShuna Spencer, founder of **KweliTV**, exemplifies this spirit of innovation. KweliTV is a streaming platform that curates and shares Black stories from around the world. By using AI algorithms to recommend content based on viewer preferences, Spencer has created a space that celebrates diversity and connects audiences with authentic narratives.

ACCESS TO CAPITAL
Overcoming Financial Barriers

Securing funding is often a major hurdle for entrepreneurs.

Challenges

- **Funding Disparities:** Black entrepreneurs receive a disproportionately small percentage of venture capital funding. Biases and lack of representation in investment firms contribute to this disparity.

- **Network Gaps:** Limited access to investor networks can hinder opportunities. Relationships often play a crucial role in securing funding, and underrepresented entrepreneurs may find themselves excluded from key circles.

Solutions

- **Alternative Funding:** Crowdfunding platforms like **Kick starter** and **Indiegogo** allow entrepreneurs to raise capital directly from the public. Grants and competitions specifi cally targeting minority-owned businesses offer additional avenues.

- **Investment Firms:** Engaging with firms dedicated to supporting Black entrepreneurs, such as **Harlem Capital** or **Backstage Capital**, which focus on investing in underrepresented founders.

- **Pitch Competitions:** Participating in events that offer funding opportunities and exposure. Competitions like **Pitch Black** provide platforms to showcase ideas to potential investors.

Consider **Stephanie Lampkin**, founder of **Blendoor**, a startup that uses AI to reduce unconscious bias in hiring. Despite initial funding challenges, Lampkin persisted and secured investments by leveraging pitch competitions and building relationships with investors who value diversity and inclusion.

BUILDING SKILLS FOR AI ENTREPRENEURSHIP
Equipping for Success

Success in AI entrepreneurship requires a combination of technical and business skills.

- **Technical Proficiency:** Understanding AI technologies and their applications is essential. This can be achieved through formal education, online courses, or self-directed learning. Platforms like **Coursera** and **Udacity** offer specialized programs in AI and machine learning.

- **Business Acumen:** Knowledge of business planning, marketing, and financial management is crucial. Resources like the **Small Business Administration (SBA)** provide guidance and tools for entrepreneurs.

- **Leadership and Management:** The ability to lead teams and manage projects ensures that ideas are executed effectively. Developing soft skills like communication, problem-solving, and adaptability enhances leadership capabilities.

LEVERAGING NETWORKS AND MENTORSHIP
The Power of Connections

Building strong networks can provide support and open doors.

- **Entrepreneurial Communities**: Joining groups like Black Founders, Startup Grind, or local startup incubators connects entrepreneurs with peers and resources.

- **Mentorship Programs**: Seeking guidance from experienced entrepreneurs and industry experts provides invaluable insights. Programs like **Mentor Makers** and **Score Mentors** offer mentorship opportunities.

- **Professional Networks**: Attending conferences and events to connect with peers and potential collaborators expands one's network. Events like **AfroTech** and **Black Tech Week** celebrate Black innovation and provide platforms for connection.

Melissa Hanna, co-founder of **Mahmee**, a maternal healthcare startup that uses AI to provide personalized care for new mothers, benefited from mentorship and networking to grow her business. By connecting with industry experts and leveraging support networks, she secured significant funding and partnerships, demonstrating the impact of strong connections.

OVERCOMING CHALLENGES
Strategies for Resilience

Entrepreneurs may face obstacles such as:

- **Access to Resources**: Limited availability of technology and infrastructure can hinder development.

- **Market Entry Barriers**: Breaking into established markets requires strategic planning and differentiation.

- **Scaling Operations:** Expanding business sustainably poses logistical and financial challenges.

Strategies to overcome these challenges include:

- **Partnerships:** Collaborating with other businesses and organizations can amplify resources and reach. Partner ships can provide access to technology, expertise, and new markets.

- **Continuous Learning:** Staying updated with the latest AI advancements ensures that businesses remain competitive. Engaging in lifelong learning through work shops, webinars, and courses is essential.

- **Community Support:** Engaging with the community to build a loyal customer base fosters sustainability. Businesses that address community needs often enjoy strong local support.

THE ROLE OF POLICY AND SUPPORT SYSTEMS
Creating an Enabling Environment

Government policies and support systems can facilitate entrepreneurship.

- **Small Business Grants:** Accessing government funding designated for small businesses through programs like the **SBA's Small Business Innovation Research (SBIR)** grants.

- **Tax Incentives:** Utilizing tax benefits for technology startups can reduce financial burdens. Credits like the **Research & Development Tax Credit** encourage innovation.

- **Incubators and Accelerators:** Joining programs that offer resources and mentorship, such as **Techstars** or **Y Combinator**, can accelerate growth and provide critical support.

FUTURE TRENDS IN AI ENTREPRENEURSHIP
Looking Ahead

Emerging trends present new opportunities.

- **AI Ethics and Fairness:** Developing AI solutions that address ethical concerns is increasingly important. Entrepreneurs can lead by creating transparent and fair AI systems.

- **Sustainability:** Integrating AI in environmental and sustainable practices opens new markets. Technologies that promote renewable energy, efficient resource use, and environmental monitoring are in demand.

- **Global Markets:** Expanding reach to international markets through AI technologies allows businesses to scale globally. Understanding cross-cultural needs and regulations is key.

Driving Innovation and Economic Impact

Entrepreneurship in the AI era offers a powerful avenue for Black Americans to drive innovation and create lasting economic impact. By leveraging AI technologies, overcoming barriers, and fostering a spirit of innovation, entrepreneurs can achieve personal success and contribute significantly to their communities and the broader economy.

Imagine a future where our neighborhoods are hubs of innovation, where businesses not only thrive economically but also address pressing social issues. A future where the next generation sees entrepreneurship as a viable and accessible path, inspired by those who came before them.

By embracing the opportunities AI presents, we take control of our narratives, build wealth within our communities, and pave the way for sustainable growth. The journey may be challenging, but with determination, support, and a commitment to innovation, the possibilities are boundless.

Let us be the architects of this future, using AI as a tool to transform our dreams into reality, and in doing so, leave a legacy of empowerment and progress for generations to come.

In the upcoming chapter, we'll delve into the critical issue of addressing bias in AI and the need for diverse voices in technology development.

By ensuring that AI systems are fair and inclusive, we can protect our communities and harness AI's full potential for good.

CHAPTER 7
Addressing Bias in AI—The Imperative for Diverse Voices

Imagine a world where technology serves everyone equally, where artificial intelligence understands and respects the rich tapestry of human diversity. Yet, as we stand on the cusp of unprecedented technological advancement, we face a critical challenge: ensuring that AI does not perpetuate the very biases we strive to overcome. For Black Americans and other marginalized communities, addressing bias in AI is not just a technical issue—it's a social imperative.

UNDERSTANDING BIAS IN AI
Unveiling the Hidden Prejudices

Artificial Intelligence learns from data, and if that data reflects societal biases, the AI systems will inadvertently perpetuate them. Bias in AI can manifest in various ways:

- **Data Bias:** When the training data is not representative of the entire population, leading to skewed outcomes. For instance, if a facial recognition system is trained predominantly on lighter-skinned faces, it may struggle to accurately recognize individuals with darker skin tones.

- **Algorithmic Bias:** When algorithms produce outputs that favor certain groups over others due to the way they're designed. This can happen even if the data is unbiased if the algorithm itself is not carefully calibrated.

- **User Interaction Bias:** When user behaviors and interactions reinforce biased outcomes. For example, if search engines present certain results based on popular but biased user queries, they can reinforce stereotypes.

IMPACT OF AI BIAS ON BLACK AMERICANS
Real-world Consequences

Biased AI systems can have detrimental effects on Black communities:

- **Criminal Justice:** Predictive policing algorithms, which are used to forecast criminal activity, may disproportionately target Black neighborhoods due to historical arrest data reflecting systemic biases. This can lead to over-policing and erosion of trust in law enforcement.

- **Employment:** AI-driven hiring tools might discriminate against applicants from certain backgrounds. If an algorithm is trained on data from a company with a history of homogenous hiring, it may favor candidates who fit that existing profile, disadvantaging qualified Black applicants.

- **Healthcare:** Diagnostic tools may be less accurate for underrepresented groups. For instance, AI models trained on data lacking diversity might fail to detect diseases in Black patients, exacerbating health disparities.

CASE STUDIES HIGHLIGHTING BIAS
Learning from Experience

Facial Recognition Issues

In 2018, a study by the Gender Shades project, led by researchers Joy Buolamwini and Timnit Gebru, revealed that several commercially available facial recognition systems had significantly higher error rates when identifying darker-skinned individuals, particularly women. While the error rate for lighter-skinned men was less than 1%, it soared to over 34% for darker-skinned women. This disparity highlighted the consequences of training AI on non-representative datasets.

Joy Buolamwini, a Black computer scientist at MIT, founded the **Algorithmic Justice League** to raise awareness about the social implications of AI biases. Her work has been instrumental in prompting companies and governments to re-evaluate and improve their facial recognition technologies.

AI in Hiring Practices

A major tech company developed an AI recruiting tool intended to streamline the hiring process by selecting top candidates from a pool of applicants. However, it was discovered that the tool was favoring male candidates over female ones. The AI had been trained on resumes submitted over a ten-year period, a time during which the tech industry was predominantly male. As a result, the algorithm learned to associate certain male-dominated terms and experiences with success, unintentionally discriminating against women.

This example underscores how AI can perpetuate existing

inequalities if not carefully monitored and adjusted to account for biases in historical data.

THE IMPORTANCE OF DIVERSE VOICES
Building Inclusive AI

Including diverse perspectives in AI development is essential to mitigate bias:

- **Improved Data Representation:** Diverse teams are more likely to recognize and address data gaps. They can ensure that training datasets are inclusive and representative of different demographics.

- **Ethical Considerations:** A variety of viewpoints contribute to more ethical decision-making. Diverse teams can anticipate how AI systems might impact various communities and work to prevent adverse effects.

- **Innovation:** Diversity fosters creativity and leads to better problem-solving. Teams with varied backgrounds can approach challenges from multiple angles, leading to more robust AI solutions.

STRATEGIES TO ADDRESS BIAS
Charting a Path Forward

Inclusive AI Development: Embracing Diversity in Tech
Companies and organizations should strive to build diverse AI teams:

- **Recruitment:** Actively seek talent from underrepresented groups. This can be achieved by partnering with historically Black colleges and universities (HBCUs), minority-serving institutions, and organizations dedicated to diversity in tech.

- **Culture:** Foster an inclusive environment where all voices are heard. Encourage open dialogue about bias and inclusivity within teams.

- **Training:** Provide education on bias and ethics in AI. Regular workshops and training sessions can help team members recognize and address potential biases in their work.

Example: Companies like IBM have established programs to promote diversity in AI development, partnering with organizations like Black Girls CODE to cultivate a new generation of diverse tech talent.

Ethical Frameworks and Standards: Guiding Principles
Implementing ethical guidelines can help steer AI development in the right direction:

- **Fairness Metrics:** Establish measurable criteria for fairness in AI systems. Regularly test algorithms for biased outcomes and adjust as necessary.

- **Transparency:** Make AI algorithms and data sources transparent for auditing. Open-source initiatives can allow external experts to examine and improve AI systems.

- **Accountability:** Hold organizations responsible for the outcomes of their AI systems. Implementing oversight committees or ethics boards can ensure ongoing compliance with ethical standards.

Example: The Partnership on AI, which includes members from academia, industry, and civil society, works to establish best practices and ethical guidelines for AI technologies.

Community Engagement: Collaborating with Those Affected
Engaging with communities that are affected by AI decisions ensures their needs are considered:

- **Feedback Mechanisms:** Create channels for users to report issues and biases. User feedback can be invaluable in identifying and correcting unintended consequences.

- **Collaborative Design:** Involve community members in the design process. Participatory design approaches can lead to AI systems that better serve diverse populations.

- **Education and Awareness:** Inform the public about AI technologies and their impacts. Empowered users are better equipped to advocate for fair and equitable AI.

Example: The AI for the People initiative, founded by Mutale Nkonde, works to educate Black communities about AI and its implications, promoting a grassroots approach to technology advocacy.

Policy and Regulation: The Role of Government
Governments can play a role in mitigating AI bias:

- **Legislation:** Enact laws that prohibit discriminatory

practices in AI applications. Regulations can set standards for fairness and accountability.

- **Standards Bodies:** Support organizations that develop ethical AI standards, such as the Institute of Electrical and Electronics Engineers (IEEE) and their work on AI ethics.

- **Funding Research:** Invest in research focused on fairness and bias mitigation. Grants and funding opportunities can spur innovation in ethical AI development.

Example: Some cities and states have implemented regulations restricting the use of biased facial recognition technology by law enforcement, acknowledging the need for oversight.

EMPOWERING BLACK VOICES IN AI
A Call to Action

Encouraging more Black individuals to enter the AI field can help reduce bias:

- **Scholarships and Grants:** Provide financial support for education in AI disciplines. Organizations like the **United Negro College Fund (UNCF)** offer scholarships specifically for STEM fields.

- **Mentorship Programs:** Connect aspiring AI professionals with mentors in the field. Programs like **Black in AI** provide mentorship, networking, and support.

- **Community Programs:** Support initiatives that introduce

AI to youth in Black communities. **Ross and Tracee Jones**, for instance, not only lead AI-driven businesses but also advocate for AI education in underserved areas, sharing their knowledge to inspire the next generation.

Building Fair and Equitable AI Systems

Addressing bias in AI is not just a technical challenge but a societal imperative. By ensuring diverse voices are included in the development and deployment of AI systems, we can create technologies that are fair, equitable, and beneficial for all.

Imagine an AI-powered healthcare system that accurately diagnoses illnesses across all populations, a criminal justice system that applies laws equitably, and educational tools that adapt to the unique learning styles of every student. This vision is attainable if we commit to inclusivity and vigilance against bias.

The active participation of Black Americans in AI is essential to dismantle systemic biases and harness AI's potential to uplift communities. By embracing diversity, advocating for ethical practices, and educating both creators and users of AI, we can shape a future where technology truly serves humanity in all its diversity.

Let us work together to ensure that the AI revolution does not repeat the injustices of the past but instead paves the way for a more just and inclusive world.

In the next chapter, we'll explore how Black innovators are already making significant contributions to AI and highlight trailblazers who are shaping the future.

Their stories serve as inspiration and a testament to the impact we can have when we embrace AI with purpose and determination.

CHAPTER 8
Building Community Through Technology

IImagine a bustling neighborhood where people of all ages gather in a local community center, not just to socialize but to engage with cutting-edge technology that strengthens their bonds. Grandparents are sharing stories through virtual reality experiences, children are exploring their cultural heritage with interactive AI-powered games, and adults are collaborating on community projects using smart platforms. This is the transformative power of technology and Artificial Intelligence (AI) in building and enhancing community ties.ac

THE ROLE OF TECHNOLOGY IN COMMUNITY BUILDING

Technology has always been a bridge connecting people, ideas, and resources. From the first telephones to today's high-speed internet, each advancement has reshaped how we interact and collaborate.

- **Communication Platforms:** Social media and messaging apps have made it effortless to stay connected with loved ones and community members, fostering a sense of belonging even when physically apart.

- **Access to Information:** Communities can now share news, events, and vital resources instantly, ensuring everyone stays informed and engaged.

- **Collaborative Projects:** Technology enables people to work together across geographical boundaries, uniting skills and passions to achieve common goals.

Consider how during times of crisis, communities have rallied together using online platforms to organize relief efforts, support local businesses, and check on the well-being of neighbors. Technology has become the heartbeat of communal resilience and solidarity.

AI-POWERED COMMUNITY SOLUTIONS

Artificial Intelligence amplifies these capabilities, offering innovative tools that can transform community engagement.

Smart Community Platforms

AI-driven platforms can revolutionize how communities interact:

- **Personalized Content:** AI algorithms can deliver relevant information to community members based on their interests and needs, ensuring that everyone receives timely and meaningful updates.

- **Facilitating Engagement:** Chatbots and AI assistants can encourage participation by answering questions, providing recommendations, and guiding users through community resources.

- **Analyzing Community Needs:** By processing data on engagement and feedback, AI can offer insights into what the community values most, helping leaders make informed decisions.

For example, a neighborhood app powered by AI might notify residents about local events they care about, suggest volunteer opportunities aligned with their interests, or even coordinate neighborhood watch programs to enhance safety.

Virtual Reality and Augmented Reality

These immersive technologies can bring communities closer:

- **Preserving Cultural Heritage:** Virtual reality can recreate historical events and significant places, allowing community members, especially the younger generation, to experience and appreciate Black history in a profound way.

- **Educational Programs:** Augmented reality can enhance learning by overlaying digital information onto the physical world, making education interactive and engaging.

- **Virtual Gatherings:** When physical meetings aren't possible, virtual reality can host gatherings that make participants feel as if they're sharing the same space, strengthening social bonds.

Imagine elders sharing stories of the civil rights movement through VR experiences, allowing others to witness history firsthand and fostering a deeper connection to their heritage.

ADDRESSING COMMUNITY CHALLENGES WITH AI

AI offers powerful tools to tackle pressing issues affecting Black communities.

Healthcare Access

AI-powered telemedicine and health apps can bridge gaps in healthcare:

- **Improving Accessibility:** Virtual consultations can bring medical expertise to underserved areas where healthcare facilities are scarce.

- **Monitoring Health Trends:** AI can analyze data to identify and address health disparities, enabling proactive interventions.

- **Personalized Care:** Health apps can offer tailored advice, medication reminders, and wellness programs that cater to individual needs.

Consider a community health initiative that uses AI to track and manage chronic conditions prevalent in the community, like hypertension or diabetes, improving overall health outcomes.

Education Enhancement
In education, AI can be a game-changer:

- **Personalized Learning:** Adaptive learning platforms can adjust content to suit each student's learning style and pace, helping them grasp concepts more effectively.

- **Supplementing Resources:** AI tutors and educational apps provide additional support outside the classroom, making quality education more accessible.

- **Bridging Gaps:** By identifying areas where students struggle, educators can address gaps promptly, reducing achievement disparities.

Imagine a student who once struggled with math now

excelling because an AI-powered app provided personalized lessons that made learning intuitive and enjoyable.

Economic Development
AI can stimulate economic growth within communities:

- **Job Matching:** AI-driven platforms can connect community members with employment opportunities that match their skills and interests.

- **Business Analytics:** Local businesses can use AI to optimize operations, understand customer behavior, and develop effective marketing strategies.

- **Financial Planning Tools:** AI-powered apps can help individuals manage finances, save for the future, and make informed investment decisions.

Picture a local entrepreneur using AI analytics to identify market trends, enabling them to expand their business and create jobs within the community.

COMMUNITY EMPOWERMENT THROUGH DATA
Data is a catalyst for positive change when used responsibly.

- **Community Surveys:** AI can analyze feedback from residents to identify priorities and concerns, ensuring that initiatives align with community needs.

- **Resource Allocation:** Data-driven insights help allocate resources effectively, whether it's planning community programs or improving infrastructure.

- **Transparency and Accountability:** Open data initiatives promote trust by keeping community members informed about decisions and progress.

An example is a city council using AI to analyze traffic patterns and community input to improve public transportation routes, enhancing accessibility for all residents.

FOSTERING COLLABORATION AND NETWORKING

AI facilitates meaningful connections:

- **Networking Platforms:** Specialized platforms can connect individuals with similar interests, fostering mentorship, collaboration, and support networks.

- **Collaborative Projects:** AI tools streamline project management, making it easier for community groups to plan events, manage volunteers, and achieve goals.

- **Mentorship Programs:** AI algorithms can match mentors with mentees based on skills, goals, and experiences, nurturing personal and professional growth.

Think of a mentorship program where experienced professionals guide youth in exploring careers in STEM fields, empowered by AI to create optimal pairings.

PROMOTING CULTURAL HERITAGE AND IDENTITY

AI technologies help preserve and celebrate culture:

- **Digital Archives:** AI can organize and digitize historical documents, photographs, and recordings, making them accessible to future generations.

- **Cultural Content Creation:** Artists can use AI to create music, art, and literature that reflect and evolve cultural identities, blending tradition with innovation.
- **Language Preservation:** AI tools can document and teach languages and dialects at risk of disappearing, keeping linguistic heritage alive.

Imagine an AI-powered app that teaches users African languages, enriched with cultural context and history, fostering a deeper connection to ancestral roots.

CHALLENGES AND ETHICAL CONSIDERATIONS

While AI offers immense benefits, mindful implementation is crucial:

- **Privacy Concerns:** Safeguarding personal data is essential. Communities must ensure that AI solutions comply with privacy laws and ethical standards.

- **Digital Literacy:** Providing education on how to use AI tools empowers community members to fully participate and benefit.

- **Equitable Access:** Efforts must be made to prevent widening the digital divide. Access to technology and the internet should be a priority.

STRATEGIES FOR SUCCESSFUL IMPLEMENTATION

Maximizing AI's benefits involves collective effort:

- **Community Involvement:** Engage residents in the planning and deployment of AI initiatives to ensure they meet real needs and have community buy-in.

- **Partnerships:** Collaborate with tech companies, educational institutions, and non-profits to bring resources and expertise into the community.

- **Education and Training:** Offer workshops and training sessions to enhance digital skills, making technology accessible to all ages.

CASE STUDY: EMPOWERING CIVIC ENGAGEMENT WITH AI

In a mid-sized city with low voter turnout, community leaders sought to increase participation in local elections. They introduced an AI-powered chatbot accessible via popular messaging apps.

"By leveraging AI chatbots, we increased community participation in local elections by 25%," reported a community organizer.

The chatbot provided:

- **Election Information:** Details on polling locations, hours, and identification requirements.

- **Candidate Platforms:** Summaries of candidates' positions on key issues, helping voters make informed decisions.

- **Reminders and Alerts:** Notifications about registration deadlines and upcoming debates or forums.

This initiative made civic participation more accessible, especially for younger voters accustomed to digital communication, and those who found traditional channels less approachable.

Strengthening Communities Through Technology

Building community through technology is a powerful way to foster unity, address shared challenges, and celebrate cultural heritage. By embracing AI, Black Americans can enhance their communities, making them more resilient, connected, and poised to thrive in the digital age.

Imagine neighborhoods where every individual feels empowered, informed, and connected—a place where technology doesn't replace human interaction but enriches it. By harnessing AI thoughtfully and inclusively, we can turn this vision into reality, ensuring that our communities not only keep pace with technological advancements but lead the way in demonstrating how technology can serve humanity.

As we move forward, the next chapter will delve into strategies for ensuring equitable access to AI technologies, addressing the digital divide, and empowering all members of our communities to participate fully in the AI-driven future.

CHAPTER 9
Case Studies—Black Innovators in AI

Imagine a world where the architects of tomorrow's technology come from all walks of life, bringing diverse perspectives that enrich and empower society as a whole. In the realm of Artificial Intelligence (AI), Black innovators are making significant strides, not only advancing the field but also ensuring that technology serves everyone equitably. Their work addresses critical issues like bias, ethics, and inclusion, laying the groundwork for a more just and innovative future.

DR. TIMNIT GEBRU
Championing Ethical AI

Dr. Timnit Gebru stands as a beacon in the AI community, renowned for her groundbreaking research on algorithmic bias and her unwavering advocacy for diversity and ethics in technology. Born in Ethiopia and immigrating to the United States at a young age, Dr. Gebru's journey is one of resilience and determination.

- **Algorithmic Bias Research:** Dr. Gebru's work has shed light on how AI systems can perpetuate and even amplify societal biases present in training data. Her research on facial recognition technologies revealed significant inaccuracies in identifying individuals with darker skin tones and women, sparking global conversations about the ethical implications of AI.

- **Diversity Advocacy:** Recognizing the lack of representation in AI, she co-founded Black in AI, an organization dedicated to increasing the presence and inclusion of Black people in the field. Through workshops, conferences, and mentorship programs, Black in AI provides support and opportunities for Black researchers and practitioners worldwide.

- **Notable Works:** Her co-authored paper, "Gender Shades: Intersectional Accuracy Disparities in Commercial Gender Classification," highlighted the racial and gender biases in commercial AI systems. This pivotal work has influenced tech companies to reassess and improve their algorithms.

> **"We need to ensure that the technologies we create do not perpetuate the inequalities that exist in our society."**
>
> — *Dr. Timnit Gebru*

Dr. Gebru's commitment to ethical AI extends beyond research. Despite facing challenges, including her controversial departure from Google in 2020 over disagreements about publishing a paper on the risks of large language models, she continues to advocate for transparency and accountability in AI development.

JOY BUOLAMWINI
The Poet of Code

Joy Buolamwini, often referred to as the "Poet of Code," is a computer scientist and digital activist whose work bridges art and technology to illuminate the social implications of AI.

- **Algorithmic Bias Discovery:** While a graduate student at MIT, Joy discovered that facial recognition software couldn't detect her face due to her darker skin tone. This personal experience led her to conduct extensive research on bias in AI systems, culminating in the influential **Gender Shades** project.

- **Advocacy and Education:** Joy founded the **Algorithmic Justice League**, an organization that combines art and research to raise awareness about the impacts of AI bias. Through documentaries, public speaking, and collaborations, she educates policymakers, industry leaders, and the public about the need for equitable AI.

- **Media and Recognition:** Featured in the acclaimed documentary "Coded Bias," Joy's work has reached global audiences. Her TED Talk, "How I'm fighting bias in algorithms," has inspired millions to consider the ethical dimensions of technology.

> **"When machines are reckless, it's people who pay the price."**
>
> — *Joy Buolamwini*

Joy's creative approach to activism, blending poetry and programming, has made complex technical issues accessible and compelling, driving meaningful change in the industry.

DR. AYANNA HOWARD
Robotics and AI Pioneer

Dr. Ayanna Howard is a distinguished roboticist, educator,

and entrepreneur whose career spans academia, industry, and social impact.

- **Academic Leadership:** As the Dean of the College of Engineering at The Ohio State University, Dr. Howard is one of the few Black women to hold such a position in a major research institution. She previously served as the Chair of the School of Interactive Computing at Georgia Institute of Technology.

- **Research Contributions:** Dr. Howard's work encompasses human-robot interaction, assistive technologies, and AI ethics. She has developed robots that can adapt to human behavior, enhancing their effectiveness in environments like disaster zones and healthcare settings.

- **Entrepreneurship:** She founded Zyrobotics, a company that creates inclusive technologies and educational products for children with diverse learning needs. By integrating AI and robotics, Zyrobotics offers interactive tools that make learning accessible and engaging.

"Diversity drives innovation—when we limit who can contribute, we in turn limit what problems we can solve."

— Dr. Ayanna Howard

Dr. Howard's dedication to mentorship and education has inspired countless students, particularly women and underrepresented minorities, to pursue careers in STEM fields.

MUTALE NKONDE
AI Policy and Advocacy

Mutale Nkonde is an AI policy advisor, researcher, and the founder of **AI For the People**, an organization aiming to educate Black communities about the social justice implications of AI.

- **Policy Work:** Nkonde has been instrumental in crafting policies that address racial bias and discrimination in technology. She has worked with U.S. congressional members on initiatives like the Algorithmic Accountability Act.

- **Public Engagement:** Through AI For the People, she creates content and programs that demystify AI and its impact on civil rights. By making complex topics accessible, she empowers communities to engage in policy discussions and advocate for ethical technology.

- **Media Presence:** Nkonde is a sought-after expert featured in outlets like The New York Times, CNN, and MIT Technology Review, where she discusses the intersection of race, technology, and policy.

Mutale's work ensures that the voices of marginalized communities are heard in conversations about AI governance and that technology advances in ways that uphold human rights.

DR. WILLIAM A. MASSEY
Mathematical Foundations of AI

Dr. William A. Massey is a pioneering mathematician whose contributions have significantly influenced the mathematical underpinnings of AI algorithms.

- **Academic Achievement:** Dr. Massey became the first African American to earn a Ph.D. in mathematics from Stanford University. He is currently a professor at Princeton University, where he continues to break new ground in his field.

- **Research Focus:** Specializing in queueing theory and stochastic processes, Dr. Massey's work is fundamental to understanding and optimizing complex systems, including those used in AI and telecommunications.

- **Mentorship:** Beyond his research, Dr. Massey is dedicated to increasing diversity in STEM fields. He co-founded the **Council for African American Researchers in the Mathematical Sciences (CAARMS)**, providing a platform for Black mathematicians to collaborate and support each other.

Dr. Massey's commitment to mentorship has opened doors for many aspiring mathematicians and AI researchers, fostering a more inclusive scientific community.

IMPACT AND LEGACY

These innovators exemplify how Black Americans are shaping the future of AI through groundbreaking research, entrepreneurship, and advocacy. Their contributions address critical issues such as:

- **Ethical AI Development:** By highlighting and combating biases in AI systems, they ensure that technology advances responsibly.

- **Representation:** Their presence and leadership in AI inspire others and bring diverse perspectives essential for innovation.

- **Community Engagement:** Through education and outreach, they bridge the gap between technological advancements and public understanding, ensuring that all communities benefit from AI.

INSPIRING THE NEXT GENERATION

The achievements of these individuals serve as beacons for the next generation of AI professionals. Their stories demonstrate that perseverance, passion, and a commitment to equity can lead to profound impacts.

Consider the words of former First Lady Michelle Obama:

"Success isn't about how much money you make; it's about the difference you make in people's lives."

Honoring Trailblazers and Building the Future

The contributions of Black innovators in AI are invaluable in driving the field forward and ensuring it serves all members of society equitably. Their work underscores the importance of diversity, ethics, and inclusion in technology.

By recognizing and supporting such trailblazers, we pave the way for a more inclusive and innovative future in AI.

Imagine a world where technology reflects the rich diversity of its creators, where AI systems are free from bias, and where innovation benefits everyone.

This vision becomes attainable when we celebrate and support those who lead the way.

Let us honor these trailblazers by continuing their legacy—advocating for diversity, striving for ethical AI, and inspiring future generations to pursue excellence in technology.

As we approach the final chapters, we will explore actionable steps for individuals and communities to embrace AI, overcome challenges, and shape a future where technology serves as a catalyst for empowerment and equality.

CHAPTER 10
Preparing the Next Generation for an AI-Driven World

Imagine a classroom buzzing with excitement as students collaborate on building their own robots, coding interactive stories, or exploring virtual reality environments. These aren't scenes from a distant future–they're happening now in schools and community centers embracing the power of technology. For Black Americans, equipping the next generation with the skills and knowledge to navigate an AI-driven world is not just an educational goal; it's a critical step toward ensuring equality, representation, and prosperity in the decades to come.

THE IMPORTANCE OF EARLY EDUCATION
Planting the Seeds of Curiosity

Introducing AI concepts at an early age fosters interest and builds foundational skills that will serve children throughout their lives.

- **STEM Curriculum Integration:** Schools should incorporate Science, Technology, Engineering, and Mathematics (STEM) into the curriculum starting from elementary levels. By making STEM subjects engaging and relatable, we can ignite a passion for learning. Programs like **STEM NOLA**, founded by Dr. Calvin Mackie, bring hands-on STEM activities to communities, making technology accessible and fun for young learners.

- **Coding for Kids:** Learning programming languages enhances problem-solving abilities and logical thinking. Platforms like Scratch, developed by MIT, allow children to create their own games and animations, fostering creativity alongside technical skills.

- **Interactive Learning:** Utilizing games and apps that teach AI and coding concepts in engaging ways can make learning feel like play. Tools like Osmo integrate physical play with digital learning, helping children grasp complex concepts intuitively.

Consider **Kimberly Bryant**, who founded **Black Girls CODE** after noticing the lack of diversity in her daughter's computer science programs. Her organization provides workshops and camps that introduce girls of color to coding and technology, empowering them to become innovators.

ROLE OF PARENTS AND GUARDIANS
Nurturing Interest and Confidence

Family involvement is crucial in nurturing a child's interest in AI and technology.

- **Encouragement:** Support children's interests in technology through positive reinforcement. Celebrate their achievements, no matter how small, to build confidence.

- **Resource Provision:** Provide access to books, kits, and online resources related to AI. Educational kits like **LittleBits** and **LEGO Mindstorms** offer hands-on experiences that make learning tangible.

- **Exposure:** Visit science museums, tech fairs, and workshops together. Experiences like the **Museum of Science and Industry** in Chicago or local maker fairs can inspire wonder and curiosity.

Parents don't need to be tech experts themselves. Showing enthusiasm and learning alongside their children can strengthen bonds and demonstrate that it's never too late to embrace new skills.

MENTORSHIP AND ROLE MODELS
Guiding Lights on the Journey

Connecting youth with mentors in the AI field can inspire and guide them toward success.

- **Mentorship Programs:** Organizations like **Mentoring in Medicine** and **Black Boys Code** offer mentorship opportunities that connect students with professionals who share similar backgrounds and experiences.

- **Networking Events:** Attending events where young people can meet AI professionals exposes them to potential career paths. Conferences like **AfroTech Junior** provide youth-focused programming within larger tech events.

- **Highlighting Success Stories:** Sharing stories of Black innovators in AI, like those highlighted in the previous chapter, motivates the youth by showing them what's possible.

For example, learning about **Dr. Mae Jemison**, the first Black woman astronaut and a strong advocate for science education, can inspire students to reach for the stars—both literally and figuratively.

ACCESS TO RESOURCES AND TECHNOLOGY
Bridging the Digital Divide

Ensuring that young people have the tools they need to learn and experiment with AI is essential.

- **Community Centers:** Establish facilities equipped with computers and internet access. Libraries and community centers can serve as hubs for technology education.

- **Device Accessibility:** Programs that provide laptops or tablets to students can make a significant difference. Initiatives like **One Laptop per Child** aim to eliminate barriers to technology access.

- **Internet Connectivity:** Advocating for affordable or free internet services in underserved areas is crucial. Programs like the **FCC's Lifeline** provide discounted internet access to low-income families.

Consider the impact of the **Detroit Community Technology Project**, which builds and maintains community wireless networks, ensuring that residents have reliable internet access for education and communication.

EXTRACURRICULAR ACTIVITIES
Learning Beyond the Classroom

Encouraging participation in activities outside the traditional classroom setting enriches learning experiences.

- **Robotics Clubs:** Joining or starting clubs that focus on building and programming robots fosters teamwork and practical application of skills. Competitions like **FIRST Robotics** inspire students through friendly competition.

- **Hackathons and Competitions:** Participating in events that challenge and develop AI skills allows students to apply what they've learned in real-world scenarios. Events like **Black Youth Hackathon** provide supportive environments for innovation.

- **Summer Camps:** Enrolling in camps that specialize in technology and AI education offers immersive experiences. Programs like **iD Tech Camps** provide courses in coding, game design, and AI.

These activities not only build technical skills but also encourage creativity, resilience, and collaboration.

HIGHER EDUCATION AND CAREER PATHWAYS
Charting the Course

Guiding students toward educational paths that lead to careers in AI ensures long-term success.

- **Scholarship Opportunities:** Seek scholarships specifically for minorities in STEM fields. Organizations like the **United Negro College Fund (UNCF)** and **Thurgood Marshall College Fund** offer financial support to deserving students.

- **Internships:** Gaining experience through internships at tech companies provides valuable industry exposure. Companies like **Microsoft, Google,** and **IBM** offer internships aimed at increasing diversity.

• **Academic Advising:** Working with counselors to plan courses and activities that align with AI careers ensures that students are on the right track. HBCUs like **Howard University** and **Morehouse College** have strong computer science programs with support networks for Black students.

COMMUNITY AND INSTITUTIONAL SUPPORT
A Collective Effort

Collective efforts can create an environment conducive to learning and growth.

• **Educational Partnerships:** Collaborations between schools, businesses, and nonprofits can provide resources and opportunities. For example, **TechBridge** partners with communities to offer technology programs that empower youth.

• **Policy Advocacy:** Advocating for policies that support funding for technology education ensures that programs have the necessary resources. Engaging with local school boards and legislators can drive change.

• **Community Programs:** Supporting initiatives that bring AI education to local communities, such as coding boot camps or tech workshops, expands access. Organizations like **Code2040** work to activate, connect, and mobilize the largest racial equity community in tech.

PROMOTING DIVERSITY AND INCLUSION IN AI EDUCATION
An Inclusive Approach

Creating an inclusive environment encourages more students to pursue AI.

- **Culturally Relevant Curriculum:** Incorporate examples and content that reflect students' backgrounds. This relevance increases engagement and shows the applicability of AI in various contexts.

- **Safe Learning Spaces:** Ensure that classrooms are welcoming and supportive for all students. Addressing stereotypes and fostering respect is key to building confidence.

- **Addressing Bias:** Train educators to recognize and miti gate biases in teaching practices. Professional development can equip teachers with the tools to support diverse learners effectively.

EMPHASIZING SOFT SKILLS
Building Well-Rounded Individuals

In addition to technical skills, soft skills are essential for success in any field.

- **Critical Thinking:** Encourage questioning and exploration of ideas. Problem-solving exercises and open discussions stimulate intellectual curiosity.

- **Collaboration:** Foster teamwork through group projects and activities. Learning to work effectively with others prepares students for collaborative work environments.

- **Communication:** Develop the ability to articulate ideas effectively. Presentations, writing assignments, and debates enhance communication skills.

Employers often seek candidates who can not only perform technical tasks but also contribute positively to team dynamics and adapt to changing circumstances.

PREPARING FOR THE FUTURE JOB MARKET
Embracing Change

Anticipating changes in the job market helps in guiding career choices.

- **Lifelong Learning:** Cultivate a mindset of continuous education and adaptability. The tech industry evolves rapidly, and staying current is essential.

- **Understanding Emerging Fields:** Stay informed about new industries and roles created by AI advancements. Fields like data science, machine learning engineering, and AI ethics offer diverse opportunities.

- **Entrepreneurial Skills:** Encourage innovation and the pursuit of entrepreneurial ventures. Programs like Junior Achievement teach business skills and inspire entrepre neurial thinking.

Imagine a young person who, inspired by their education and experiences, develops an AI application that addresses a community need, like improving access to healthy food or enhancing public safety. By preparing them now, we empower them to make meaningful contributions in the future.

Empowering the Next Generation

Preparing the next generation for an AI-driven world is a collective responsibility that requires the commitment of families, educators, communities, and policymakers.

By providing education, resources, and support, we can empower young Black Americans to not only participate in but also lead the technological advancements of the future. Investing in our youth ensures a legacy of innovation, equity, and prosperity for generations to come. As we nurture their talents and ambitions, we lay the foundation for a future where technology serves as a tool for empowerment and positive change.

Let us envision a future where the leaders in AI and technology reflect the diversity of our society, bringing unique perspectives that drive innovation and address global challenges. By acting today, we can make this vision a reality.

In the final chapter, we will bring together the themes and insights from this journey, outlining a roadmap for embracing AI as a catalyst for empowerment, innovation, and equity within Black communities and beyond.

CHAPTER 11
Seizing the Moment for a Brighter Future

IImagine standing at the edge of a vast horizon, where the sun is rising to unveil a landscape filled with possibilities. This is where we find ourselves today—the dawn of an AI-driven era that holds immense potential to transform our lives, our communities, and our future. Throughout this journey, we've explored the rich tapestry of history, the challenges we've faced, and the opportunities that lie before us. Now, it's time to bring these threads together and weave a vision for a brighter future.

THE URGENCY OF NOW
Embracing the AI Revolution

The AI revolution is not a distant phenomenon looming on the horizon; it's here, reshaping industries, economies, and societies in real-time. For Black Americans, this moment is pivotal. The decisions we make today will determine whether we are mere spectators or active architects of the future.

Every moment of hesitation is a missed opportunity to influence the trajectory of this powerful technology. Engaging with AI now means:

- **Shaping Ethical Standards:** By participating in AI development, we ensure that the technologies reflect our values and uphold principles of fairness and justice.

- **Addressing Community Needs:** We can create AI

- **Building Economic Strength:** Embracing AI opens doors to entrepreneurship, high-demand careers, and economic empowerment.

As civil rights leader John Lewis once said:

"If not us, then who? If not now, then when?"

The urgency is real, and the time to act is now.

EMPOWERMENT THROUGH PARTICIPATION
Becoming Creators and Innovators

Active participation in AI is more than learning to code or understanding algorithms; it's about taking ownership of our future. By becoming creators, innovators, and decision-makers in AI, we can:

- **Influence Ethical Standards:** Our involvement ensures diverse perspectives are considered, reducing biases and promoting inclusivity in AI systems.

- **Address Community Needs:** We can develop technologies that solve specific problems in areas like healthcare, education, and economic development within our communities.

- **Build Economic Strength:** AI offers pathways to lucrative careers and entrepreneurial ventures that can uplift individuals and stimulate community growth.

Consider the journey of **Ross and Tracee Jones**, who saw the potential of AI and founded **CommercialRealEstateMarketing.com, The CRE Marketing Hub**, and **ContentCreationStudios.us.** By leveraging AI to create realistic, diverse images and custom tools for industries like commercial real estate, they not only built successful businesses but also provided solutions that reflect and serve our communities.

COLLECTIVE ACTION AND COLLABORATION
Amplifying Our Impact

No individual can effect monumental change alone. Our strength lies in unity and collective effort. By working together, we can:

- **Strengthen Educational Initiatives:** Support and expand programs that teach AI and technology skills to all age groups.

- **Advocate for Policy Changes:** Influence legislation that promotes diversity, equity, and inclusion in technology sectors.

- **Foster Community Innovation:** Encourage and support local projects that utilize AI for social good, such as community health initiatives or educational platforms.

Organizations like **Black in AI** and **AfroTech** exemplify how collective action can create networks of support, mentorship, and opportunity. By pooling resources and sharing knowledge, we amplify our impact and drive meaningful change.

OVERCOMING CHALLENGES
Turning Obstacles into Opportunities

The path forward is not without obstacles. Systemic barriers, resource limitations, and biases persist. However, our history is a testament to resilience and perseverance. We've overcome insurmountable odds before, and we can do it again.

- **Acknowledging the Challenges:** Recognize the systemic issues that create disparities in education, access, and representation in AI.

- **Strategic Addressing:** Develop targeted strategies to overcome these barriers, such as advocating for equitable funding in education or creating platforms that highlight and combat AI bias.

- **Leveraging Community Strengths:** Utilize our rich cultural heritage, creativity, and communal bonds to find innovative solutions.

As Dr. Martin Luther King Jr. reminded us:

"We must accept finite disappointment but never lose infinite hope."

Every challenge is an opportunity for growth and transformation.

VISION FOR A BRIGHTER FUTURE
Envisioning What's Possible

Imagine a future where:

- **Educational Equity:** Every child, regardless of zip code or socioeconomic status, has access to quality AI and technology education.

- **Economic Empowerment:** Black-owned businesses flourish by integrating AI, creating jobs, and stimulating economic growth within our communities.

- **Social Justice:** AI systems are free from bias, contributing to fair treatment in criminal justice, hiring practices, healthcare, and more.

- **Cultural Preservation:** Technology is harnessed to celebrate, preserve, and share Black history and culture, enriching our collective identity.

This is not just a dream—it's a reachable goal. But it requires collective action, strategic planning, and unwavering commitment.

CALL TO ACTION
Steps Toward Empowerment

The responsibility lies with each of us to take actionable steps:

- **Educate Yourself:** Seek out resources to understand AI

and its implications. Online courses, workshops, and community programs are more accessible than ever.

- **Get Involved:** Participate in community initiatives focused on technology. Volunteer, join local tech groups, or start a club.

- **Support Others:** Mentor, teach, and inspire the next generation. Share your knowledge and experiences to uplift others.

- **Advocate for Change:** Use your voice to promote policies and practices that foster inclusion. Engage with local leaders, vote, and raise awareness.

Consider starting with small, tangible actions. Attend a local tech meetup, enroll in an online AI course, or mentor a young person interested in technology. Every step counts.

EMBRACING THE JOURNEY AHEAD
A Collective Commitment

The journey toward a future where Black Americans are fully integrated into the AI landscape is ongoing. It's a marathon, not a sprint, requiring perseverance, adaptability, and collective effort.

- **Stay Informed:** Keep abreast of technological advancements and their societal impacts.

- **Build Networks:** Connect with others who share your vision. Collaboration multiplies our efforts.

- **Celebrate Successes:** Acknowledge and honor the achievements within our communities. Success stories inspire and motivate others.

Let us draw inspiration from trailblazers like **Dr. Timnit Gebru, Joy Buolamwini**, and **Dr. Ayanna Howard**, who have made significant strides in AI while advocating for diversity and ethics.

FINAL THOUGHTS
Embracing the Future Together

As we stand on the precipice of this new era, let us remember that the story doesn't end here. This is the beginning of a transformative journey that we embark on together.

THE POWER OF UNITY
Our collective efforts have the power to reshape industries, influence policies, and redefine societal norms. By uniting, we can:

- **Share Knowledge:** Create platforms and networks where information and resources are exchanged freely.

- **Support Each Other:** Offer mentorship, encouragement, and assistance to those pursuing careers or ventures in AI.

- **Advocate for Change:** Present a united front in influencing policies and practices that promote inclusivity and fairness in technology.

CONTINUING THE CONVERSATION

The dialogue around AI and its implications for Black Americans must persist beyond these pages. Ongoing conversations ensure that we remain informed, proactive, and engaged.

- **Community Forums:** Participate in discussions at local community centers, churches, or online platforms.

- **Educational Workshops:** Attend and organize events that focus on AI literacy and its societal impacts.
- **Social Media Engagement:** Use platforms like Twitter, LinkedIn, and Facebook to share insights, news, and opportunities related to AI.

A VISION FOR TOMORROW

Envision a world where technology serves as a tool for equality, empowerment, and positive change—a world where our contributions to AI are not the exception but the norm. By actively shaping the narrative around AI, we ensure that it reflects the diversity and richness of our experiences. This vision becomes a reality when we commit to action, support one another, and remain steadfast in our pursuit of progress.

FINAL ENCOURAGEMENT
Be the Catalyst

Embracing AI is a journey filled with learning, challenges, and growth. While obstacles may arise, remember that each of us has the power to effect change. Your unique perspective, skills, and voice are invaluable in this collective effort. Let the words of Nelson Mandela inspire you:

"It always seems impossible until it's done."

Believe in your ability to make a difference. Take that first step, and then another. Encourage others to join you. Together, we can and will create a future where technology enhances our lives and propels us toward greater achievements.

As we conclude this exploration, let us carry forward the insights gained, the challenges identified, and the possibilities envisioned. The story of Black Americans embracing AI is still being written, and each of us holds a pen.

Thank you for embarking on this journey. May it ignite a passion for innovation within you, foster collaboration, and inspire action. The future is not just something that happens to us—it's something we create. Let's seize this moment and build a brighter, more inclusive future together.

This is not the end but a new beginning.

Embrace the possibilities, take action, and be a part of shaping the world we all aspire to live in.

ABOUT THE AUTHOR

Fondly referred to as "the Godfather of Digital Marketing for CRE," Ross Jones has been credited for introducing digital marketing trends and strategies to the commercial real estate industry, driving lead generation, branding, and promotion efforts.

His expertise led to a new agent winning Best of Market in her first year, and he has ignited a movement within the CRE industry, collectively generating over $1 billion in leads for CRE agents. Committed to leveraging technology for industry advancement, Ross began working with AI technologies in 2020, three years before the release of ChatGPT and mainstream AI adoption. He created the first AI tools for CRE training, marketing, and mentoring available to the public.

Ross is the Co-founder of CommercialRealEstateMarketing.com, home to the CRE Marketing Hub—the first platform offering GPTs specifically designed for CRE agents.

This groundbreaking platform equips commercial real estate professionals with AI tools, prompts, and calculators to streamline their marketing and business operations, revolutionizing the way CRE professionals leverage technology.

With over 12 years of experience, Ross has built a diverse client base across the United States, working with real estate agents, executives, and business owners to provide expertise in video coaching, lead generation, and AI integration —enhancing visibility, streamlining systems, and driving revenue.

As a national speaker and author, Ross continues to shape the future of the commercial real estate industry through innovation, technology, and education.

To connect with Ross or invite to speak at your event, visit www.CommercialRealEstateMarketing.com/book-a-speaker

RESOURCES

UNLOCKING THE POWER OF AI
Essential Tools for Every Aspect of Life

Artificial Intelligence is no longer a distant concept—it's a practical tool shaping how we create, work, learn, and live. This resource section is designed to empower you with the most impactful AI tools across various industries and applications. Whether you're a creative visionary, a business professional, a lifelong learner, or a community advocate, these tools will help you harness the transformative power of AI.

From platforms that fuel creativity to those driving productivity, education, data insights, and social change, this curated list includes something for everyone. Each tool is paired with a brief description, making it easy for you to explore and integrate these technologies into your personal and professional life.

Embrace these tools, and take the next step toward building a future where AI works for you. Let's dive into the possibilities!

AI TOOLS FOR CREATIVITY

- **MidJourney:** A leading AI platform for generating high-quality art and visuals from text prompts.
- **Runway ML:** A tool designed for creators, offering features like video editing, image generation, and custom AI model training.
- **DALL-E 3:** An OpenAI tool for creating detailed and imaginative images from textual descriptions.
- **Jasper AI:** A writing assistant for content creators, marketers, and businesses.
- **Suno:** An AI tool for creating immersive soundscapes, music, and audio content.
- **Ideogram:** A cutting-edge platform for generating creative visual designs and text-based art.

AI TOOLS FOR BUSINESS & PRODUCTIVITY

- **ChatGPT:** A conversational AI for generating ideas, answering questions, and automating tasks.
- **Notion AI:** Enhances productivity by integrating AI features into task management, documentation, and collaboration workflows.
- **Zapier AI Integration:** Automates workflows by connecting apps and triggering actions using AI-based rules.
- **Synthesia:** Allows businesses to create AI-powered video content with customizable avatars and voices.
- **Gamma:** An AI tool for creating visually stunning and interactive presentations effortlessly.
- **HeyGen:** A platform for generating AI-driven video presentations and explainer content.
- **Otter.ai:** Transcribes meetings and conversations in real time, making collaboration seamless.

AI TOOLS FOR EDUCATION & SKILL BUILDING
- **ChatGPT:** A versatile AI tool for learning, brainstorming, and answering questions in real time, making it a powerful tutor and research assistant.
- **Perplexity.ai:** An AI-powered search assistant that provides clear, concise answers and sources for deeper learning.
- **Coursera:** Offers AI and machine learning courses from top universities and institutions worldwide.
- **OpenAI Codex:** Assists with coding and programming by translating natural language into code.
- **Duolingo Max:** An AI-powered language learning assistant.
- **EdX:** Offers cutting-edge courses in AI, data science, and other key topics from top-tier institutions.
- **Skillshare:** Features AI-powered creative and professional skill-building courses taught by experts.
- **Google Bard:** A tool for advanced research, creative brainstorming, and real-time knowledge exploration.
- **LinkedIn Learning:** Provides AI-powered recommendations for professional development courses, including AI and emerging technologies.

AI TOOLS FOR ANALYTICS & DATA SCIENCE
- **DataRobot:** Streamlines AI development and deployment for data-driven decision-making.
- **Tableau:** Leverages AI to help users visualize and analyze data trends effectively.
- **Hugging Face:** A hub for sharing and deploying AI models, particularly in natural language processing.

AI TOOLS FOR SOCIAL GOOD
- **AI for the People:** Educates underrepresented communities about AI's societal impacts.
- **Data for Black Lives:** Uses data science and AI to address social justice issues.
- **Algorithmic Justice League:** Focuses on combating biases in AI systems.

AI TOOLS FOR EVERYDAY USE
- **Grammarly:** An AI-driven writing assistant for improving grammar, style, and clarity.
- **Otter.ai:** Transcribes meetings and conversations in real time.
- **Canva AI:** Integrates AI tools for graphic design, including image suggestions and layout adjustments.
- **Perplexity.ai:** An AI-powered search and question-answering tool designed for quick, reliable information retrieval.

AI TOOLS FOR BUDGETING, MONEY MANAGEMENT, AND INVESTING
Managing your finances and growing your wealth can be complex, but AI tools are here to simplify the process. From budgeting to investing, these platforms provide actionable insights and automation to help you achieve your financial goals.

For Budgeting and Money Management

- **Mint:** A widely used app for managing personal finances, tracking spending, and setting budgets with smart AI-driven recommendations.

- **YNAB (You Need A Budget):** A budgeting tool that uses AI to help users assign every dollar a job, ensuring they meet financial goals.
- **PocketGuard:** AI-powered app that shows how much disposable income you have after accounting for bills, goals, and necessities.
- **Plum:** An AI assistant that helps users save money automatically by analyzing spending habits and rounding up transactions.
- **Goodbudget:** Digital envelope budgeting with AI to allocate funds and track spending habits effectively.

For Investing

- **Betterment AI:** AI-powered robo-advisor for goal-based investing and portfolio optimization.
- **Wealthfront AI:** Uses AI for automated investing, tax-loss harvesting, and personalized savings plans.
- **Acorns AI:** Automatically rounds up purchases and invests spare change using AI-powered algorithms.
- **Personal Capital AI Tools:** Offers AI-driven insights for portfolio tracking and investment optimization.
- **Fidelity AI Portfolio Insights:** Uses AI to assess portfolio risks and provide tailored investment recommendations.
- **Robinhood AI Features:** Real-time stock analysis and AI-powered market insights for DIY investing.

AI TOOLS FOR WRITING AND PUBLISHING

Writing a book or publishing your work has never been easier thanks to advancements in AI. From brainstorming ideas to formatting and marketing, these tools empower authors to focus on their creativity while leaving the heavy lifting to AI.

For Writing

- **Sudowrite:** This AI tool helps authors brainstorm ideas, refine prose, and expand descriptions. Whether you're stuck on dialogue or need inspiration for a plot twist, Sudowrite has your back.
- **Jasper AI:** Jasper assists with generating content, maintaining tone consistency, and providing creative prompts, making it an invaluable tool for storytelling.
- **Grammarly:** Beyond catching grammar errors, Grammarly uses AI to enhance style, tone, and clarity, helping authors polish their manuscripts.
- **NovelAI:** Tailored for fiction writers, NovelAI generates ideas for characters, plots, and world-building to fuel your imagination.
- **ChatGPT:** A versatile assistant that helps with brainstorming plotlines, crafting dialogue, and conducting research for your book.
- **StoryLab.ai:** This tool specializes in generating storylines and exploring themes, offering endless creative possibilities.

For Publishing

- **Reedsy AI Features:** A platform with AI-enhanced tools to refine formatting and editing, making your book professional and market-ready.
- **Atticus.io:** An AI-powered book formatting tool designed for eBooks and print publishing.
- **KDP (Kindle Direct Publishing) with AI Tools:** Amazon's publishing platform offers AI features to optimize your manuscript for Kindle and print.

- **Canva AI**: An intuitive platform that integrates AI to create stunning book covers, promotional graphics, and social media assets.
- **Speechify AI**: This AI-driven audiobook narrator converts your text into lifelike audio, making audiobook production affordable and efficient.

THE FUTURE IS NOW

These AI tools represent just the beginning of what's possible when technology and creativity intersect. Whether you're writing your first novel, preparing to self-publish, or taking steps toward financial independence, AI empowers you to achieve your goals more efficiently and effectively.

By integrating these tools into your workflow, you can focus on what truly matters—creating, building, and investing in a future you're passionate about. Remember, the potential of AI is limitless, and the best time to start leveraging it is now.